Table of Contents

Chapter 1 – Introduction

This manual describes PC Tools Deluxe, a disk and file utility program, and also the supplementary programs PCBackup, PCRestor, Compress, PC–Cache, PCFormat, Mirror and Rebuild. These programs are for IBM Personal computers and compatibles.

PC Tools Deluxe supports all models of the IBM PC, PS/2 (it includes both 3–1/2 and 5–1/4 inch diskettes), and most compatibles. You can use it with any version of DOS 2.0 or higher. (However, we recommend that AT&T, Compaq, and Burroughs owners read the section titled "AT&T, Burroughs, & Compaq computers" as some of these DOS versions have a destructive hard disk format.)

PC Tools Deluxe provides many of the same features found in DOS such as the ability to copy files or an entire disk, rename files, and delete files. Combined with these additional features for recovering files that have been accidentally deleted, viewing the contents of any file, locating files on the disk, finding specific text on a disk or in selected files and much more.

PC Tools Deluxe is also designed to stay "resident" in the computer's memory while other programs are running. This means that you can call up PC Tools Deluxe at any time from within other programs, to format new disks, copy files, etc. Then, when you're finished using PC Tools Deluxe, you can return to the original program.

PC Tools Deluxe includes these features:

WORD PROC   Create and edit documents even while running other programs.

DIRECTORY   Maintenance features allow you to sort, create, remove, rename, and "prune and graft" your subdirectories.

PC Tools Deluxe

COPY   Copy a file, groups of files, or an entire disk.

MOVE   Just like copying files but it will delete the
                  source file(s) copied.

COMPARE   Compare file(s) or entire disk(s).

FIND   Search a file, a group of files, or an entire
                  disk for a matching string of data.

RENAME   Rename a file or volume label.

DELETE   Delete a file or a group of files.

VERIFY   Verify that all sectors are readable in a file, or
                  group of files. Will also verify an entire disk
                  allowing unused bad sectors to be removed
                  from available use.

VIEW/EDIT   View and/or modify data in a file or on a
                  disk.

UNDELETE   Attempt recovery of deleted files and
                  subdirectories and their data.

ATTRIBUTE   Display (and optionally modify) the directory
                  status of files and/or the files' time and date.

SORT   Sort files by name, extension, size or
                  date/time.

MAPPING   Display the allocation of the sectors on a
                  disk and display the allocation for individual
                  files.

SYSTEM INFO   Display helpful information about your
                  system.

PRINT   Print files.

LOCATE   Search all directories for specific files.

INITIALIZE   Format a data diskette.

PARK   Safely stores the drive head for safe
                     transportation of your computer.

Also on your PC Tools Deluxe disk are these other disk utilities:

COMPRESS   Analyze a hard disk or floppy diskette for
                     fragmentation and optionally correct it.

PCBACKUP   Make floppy diskette archival backups of your
                     hard disk files.

PCRESTOR   Restore hard disk files from floppy diskette
                     backups made with PCBACKUP.

PC–CACHE   Improve disk performance by storing
                     frequently used information in the computer's
                     memory.

PC–FORMAT   A safe Format program for hard and floppy
                     disks. Creates disks that can be Unformatted
                     by Rebuild.

MIRROR and   Recover from accidental format of your
REBUILD   hard disk. Improve Undelete reliability.

About This Manual

This manual will show you how to use each option step–by–step.
In nearly every case, PC Tools Deluxe will show "reminder"
prompts as to what commands or menu options are valid. We

encourage you to carefully read through this manual to take advantage of all of PC Tools Deluxe's features. This manual is divided into eight chapters, an appendix and an index:

Chapter One is an introduction to PC Tools Deluxe and its features.

Chapter Two shows you how to install PC Tools Deluxe to a hard disk.

Chapter Three explains each option of PC Tools Deluxe in depth.

Chapter Four describes the utility program COMPRESS which will optimize a disk's performance and monitor it for bad clusters, locking them out before DOS uses them.

Chapter Five documents PCBACKUP and PCRESTOR, programs that make fast, reliable hard disk backups.

Chapter Six shows you how to use MIRROR and REBUILD, and PCFORMAT to protect against an accidental FORMAT of your disks.

Chapter Seven describes PC–CACHE, a program to speed up disk access by storing frequently used information in the computer's memory.

Chapter Eight has a listing of all error messages generated by the PC Tools programs and a description of what they mean.

An appendix at the end of the manual describes the other software backup and utility products from Central Point Software.

An index will help you locate specific sections if you are having difficulty or can't find the information you need.

Hardware Requirements

PC Tools Deluxe is designed to work with the IBM PS/2 (all models) PC, PCjr (256K), XT, AT, and most IBM–compatible computers. Your computer should have at least 256K of memory. If you wish to keep PC Tools Deluxe "resident" in memory while other programs are running, it's a good idea to have 512K or more memory. You need only one disk drive, though PC Tools Deluxe can also work with multiple disk drives, including hard disks and RAMdisks.

To start up PC Tools Deluxe, you need to boot your computer with version 2.0 (or higher) of DOS. Once PC Tools Deluxe is running, it can work with disks formatted by any version of DOS.

NOTE: We have made a great effort to make PC Tools Deluxe compatible with other resident programs such as Prokey™ and Sidekick™. PC Tools Deluxe is very "well–behaved" in it's operation while some other resident programs are not. If you experience any problems with PC Tools Deluxe and other resident programs, try changing the order in which your resident programs are loaded. (We'd also appreciate knowing which programs you had trouble with.)

What You Need to Know

PC Tools Deluxe can act as a replacement for the following internal and external DOS commands: COMP, COPY, DIR, DISKCOMP, DISKCOPY, ERASE, FORMAT, RENAME, TREE, TYPE, VER, CHDIR, MKDIR, RMDIR, ATTRIB, LABEL, VOL, BACKUP and RESTORE.

To use PC Tools Deluxe, we assume that you are generally familiar with MS–DOS or IBM PC–DOS, and know about files, filenames and extensions, and how to use the common DOS commands. You should know how to boot DOS (answering the

PC Tools Deluxe

date and time questions if necessary) to get to the DOS "A>" prompt. If you need to know more about these things, you should refer to your IBM Disk Operating System manual.

If you wish to make extensive use of the VIEW/EDIT or FIND options, an understanding of ASCII characters and hexadecimal numbers is also helpful.

Getting Started

If you bought this product from your local dealer or from a mail order company, fill out and send in your registration card now. Being a registered owner entitles you to technical support, should you need it, and it lets us tell you about product updates. When we enhance or update the PC Tools Deluxe program in the future (which is done on a regular basis), all registered owners are able to purchase the update at a reduced price. (If you purchased your PC Tools Deluxe directly from Central Point Software, you are already registered as an owner – you don't need to return a registration card.)

PC Tools Deluxe is not copy–protected in any way. You can back it up using the PC Tools Deluxe COPY DISK option, the DOS COPY command, or any other standard disk copy program. We encourage you to make a backup copy and put your original PC Tools Deluxe disk in a safe place.

The PC Tools Deluxe disk comes to you without DOS. You can either boot from a DOS disk before inserting the PC Tools Deluxe disk, **or you can use the PCSETUP program supplied on the disk (see the next chapter) to transfer all the files to their own subdirectory on a hard disk and make all the additions to your AUTOEXEC.BAT file for you automatically.**

Chapter 2 – Installing to a Hard Disk

While PC Tools Deluxe can be used with a floppy disk system, it really excels when you have a hard disk. In addition, several of its functions are designed specifically to be used with a hard disk, such as PCBACKUP and PCRESTOR.

PC SETUP

To set up PC Tools Deluxe on a hard disk:

1. Remove any previous PC Tools Deluxe files and subdirectory from the hard disk (including files *.cfg and *.ovl in the root directory).

2. Boot the computer with an **unmodified DOS disk** from drive A.

3. Remove the DOS disk and insert PC Tools Deluxe in drive A.

4. At the A> type: PCSETUP and press enter.

5. Follow the instructions on the screen for installing resident programs.

6. Reboot the computer. You are now ready to begin using all of the PC Tools Deluxe options.

Note: "Menu" programs etc., can interfere with PCSETUP, not allowing the PC Tools Deluxe programs to be properly installed although they do appear in the autoexec.bat file. If the programs do not execute properly after rebooting, make sure the computer was booted with an unmodified DOS disk from drive A, before PCSETUP was run.

The PC SETUP program will copy all of the PC Tools Deluxe programs to a subdirectory on your hard disk. It will also

PC Tools Deluxe

optionally install MIRROR in your AUTOEXEC.BAT file to protect against accidental FORMAT of your hard disk, add a PATH statement so DOS can always find the PC Tools Deluxe programs, add PC–Cache to your system, and install PC Tools Deluxe in your AUTOEXEC file so it is resident and available every time you turn on your computer.

PCSETUP will also look for FORMAT.COM programs in the root directory and in all PATHS on your hard disk and rename them to FORMAT!.COM. It will create a batch file called FORMAT.BAT that will run PCFORMAT anytime you type FORMAT. This allows you to recover both your hard and floppy disks from accidental formatting. If you ever want to run the original DOS format program, type: FORMAT! instead of FORMAT.

If for any reason you wish to change the setup options made by PCSETUP, use the PC Tools Deluxe Word Processor to edit your AUTOEXEC.BAT file.

Chapter 3 – Using PC Tools Deluxe

The PC Tools Deluxe Program

Here is a short description of PC Tools Deluxe and its options, following the notation of the IBM DOS manual:

PCTOOLS Command

Purpose: Provides a number of useful DOS options from a single program, including the ability to recover deleted files and examine disk sectors.

Format: PCTOOLS [/BW] [/RnnnK] [/Fn] [/Od]

Remarks:

The /BW parameter provides a clearer display if you have a black–and–white or single–color monitor connected to a color graphics adapter. (If you have a monochrome display board, PC Tools Deluxe will display in black–and–white automatically.) If your screen is difficult to read, and you don't have a color display select this option. If you used PCSETUP to install PC Tools Deluxe and you have this problem, edit your AUTOEXEC file with PC Tools Deluxe's Word Processor and add the /BW option to the PC Tools command line.

The /RnnnK parameter installs PC Tools Deluxe as a resident program, so that it can be used at any time, including from within other programs. The "nnn" represents how many Kilobytes of memory should be set aside for the PC Tools Deluxe program and memory buffers. This number must be at least 64, as in "/R64K", to provide 64K of memory for PC Tools Deluxe. If you have a 20 megabyte or larger hard disk, the minimum memory will probably be approximately 75K (e.g. "/R75k").

PC Tools Deluxe

The best number to use for the /R option depends on several things. There is a "Recommended /R Settings" table to help you select an optimum /R value for your computer system. If you used PCSETUP, it already picked the recommended /R value for you. Here are all the details of how PC Tools Deluxe uses memory:

1. The smallest allowable value is 64K.
2. The number should be at least 128K less than the amount of available user memory in your computer after booting DOS. Bring up PC Tools Deluxe without the "/RxxxK" parameter and use the "System Info" option from the "Disk and Special Functions" menu to determine the available user memory and the memory used by DOS and other resident programs. For example, if your computer has 640K of memory, then the largest number you can use for PC Tools Deluxe is 512K minus the memory used by DOS and other resident programs.
3. If you have only one disk drive, then using a smaller number means that PC Tools Deluxe will require more disk swaps when copying or comparing between disks.
4. Conversely, the larger the number, the less memory space is available for your other programs.
5. Any number less than 177K will force PC Tools Deluxe to create an "overlay" file. This file contains much of the program code for PC Tools Deluxe. The advantage of an overlay file is that PC Tools Deluxe can be made resident in less memory than it takes to hold the entire PC Tools Deluxe program and its buffers.
6. PC Tools Deluxe supports the Lotus/Intel/Microsoft Expanded Memory Standard. Therefore, if you have an Above Board or equivalent memory expansion board, any overlay file that would be created will instead use expanded memory. PC Tools Deluxe will also use expanded memory to increase buffer space so disk swaps will be kept to a minimum.
7. If you determine after you have been running for a while that you would like to remove the resident PC Tools Deluxe program and free the memory that it occupies, be sure that you are at the DOS "A>" prompt, not within another program, and use CTRL–ESC to go to the PC Tools Deluxe

"File Functions" menu. Press F3 to go to the "Disk and Special Functions" menu. Then press CTRL–F3 and PC Tools Deluxe will check to see if it thinks it is wise to free up the memory. If other programs like Sidekick™ or even the DOS PRINT command are used, they may be made resident AFTER PC Tools Deluxe. <u>You should NOT let PC Tools Deluxe free up its memory if other programs were made resident after PC Tools Deluxe.</u> Or unpredictable results may occur and you might have to reboot your computer. PC Tools will ask for confirmation to proceed.

8. <u>Recommended /R Settings:</u>

Here are some settings we have found work well for various computer configurations with version 4.00 and up of PC Tools Deluxe:

```
PCTOOLS          (to run non–resident)
PCTOOLS /R75K    (to run resident from a 10 meg hard disk)
PCTOOLS /R80K    (to run resident from a 20 meg hard disk)
PCTOOLS /R85K    (to run resident from a 30 meg hard disk)
PCTOOLS /R177K   (to run resident on a floppy disk system)
PCTOOLS /R64K    (to run resident on a PC with less than
                 256K)
```

Note: If PC Tools Deluxe tells you it does not have enough memory in resident mode, try increasing the "/Rnnn" number by 5K. This should correct the problem (it can occur if you have a large hard disk, lots of subdirectories, or lots of files in any subdirectory.)

<u>The /O parameter</u> will force an overlay file regardless of the amount of memory specified and regardless of whether the program was or was not made resident. This can be helpful if you want to assign PC Tools Deluxe 177K or more memory and want it to maximize its buffer size to avoid disk swaps. You can also specify the drive to create the overlay file on (e.g. "/OC" will create the overlay file on drive "C" regardless of where PC Tools

Deluxe was started from). This is most beneficial on systems with a single drive (and possibly a RAM disk) but no expanded memory. If you omit the drive or if it is invalid, the default drive will be used.

The /Fn parameter can change the keys used to activate PC Tools Deluxe from CTRL–ESC to CTRL–Fn, where Fn is any one of the function keys (F11 and F12 on the newer IBM keyboards are not supported). This is useful if another program you run, such as Prokey™, also uses CTRL–ESC. Use the /Fn option when starting PC Tools Deluxe, replacing the "n" with a number from 1 to 10 to designate which function key to use. For example,

```
PCTOOLS /R75K /F6
```

will load PC Tools Deluxe and make it a resident program, with an overlay file created on the current DOS drive. CTRL–F6 will activate it instead of CTRL–ESC.

Once PC Tools Deluxe is installed as a resident program, it can be started at any time by pressing CTRL–ESC. If a "DOS function" is executing, there will be a short pause while the function is completed, before the PC Tools Deluxe "File Functions" menu appears. When you exit out of the resident PC Tools Deluxe, you're returned to the interrupted program.

Running PC Tools Deluxe "Resident"

PC Tools Deluxe can be made "resident" in memory, harmlessly "lurking" in the background while other programs are running. If you used PCSETUP to install PC Tools Deluxe on your hard disk, it may already be resident and ready for you to use. To use PC Tools Deluxe resident, we recommend that you have at least 512K of memory in your computer.

1. If you do not have a hard disk or have not run PCSETUP,
   insert your PC Tools Deluxe disk into drive A. If you have
   already run PCSETUP, skip ahead to number "3".

2. Type "pctools /r75k":

```
A>pctools /r75k
```

The "/r" means "resident" and the "75K" indicates how much
memory to set aside for the PC Tools Deluxe program and
temporary storage.

The disk will whir as the PC Tools Deluxe program is loaded
from disk into the computer's memory, then this message will
appear:

```
Building overlay file using path,
C:\
PC Tools Deluxe RX.xx installed.

A>
```

Your computer will work just like it always does, with two
exceptions:

Your programs will not have as much memory to work with, since
PC Tools Deluxe is occupying some of the computer's memory
(until you reboot again or remove PC Tools Deluxe from your
computer's memory).

You can now start up PC Tools Deluxe at any time, even from
within other programs. Note: PC Tools Deluxe does not
support programs running in EGA graphics mode.

3. Press CTRL–ESC (Press and hold down the CTRL key, then
   press the ESC key).

A PC Tools Deluxe sign–on screen will appear. Press any key to see the "File Functions" menu. From here you can select any of the options of PC Tools Deluxe.

4. Press CTRL–ESC again (or press ESC. Answer "Y" to the "Are you SURE you want to exit PC Tools Deluxe" question).

The original display (before you typed CTRL–ESC) reappears, as if nothing had happened.

5. Start up one of your other programs, such as a word processor, spreadsheet, etc., while PC Tools Deluxe is resident. (Don't press CTRL–ALT–DEL, or you will lose the resident PC Tools Deluxe.) Once your program is running, type CTRL–ESC again. The PC Tools Deluxe "File Functions" menu will come back. (There may be a short pause first if your program was busy performing a "DOS function".)

After you make PC Tools Deluxe resident, it is always ready to go, to provide a number of useful functions. Each of the PC Tools Deluxe options is explained later in this chapter.

6. Exit out of the PC Tools Deluxe program again. The program you were running before will return to the screen.

Note: The process of starting up PC Tools Deluxe as a resident program may disable the DOS ASSIGN command.

Scrolling the "File Functions" Display

PC Tools Deluxe will normally display the first 26 files on the two column display ("F2" will switch back and forth to a 13 file single column display with expanded information. Try it). In order to perform one of the options on a given file, you indicate that given file by positioning the inverse or colored bar over that file and pressing the option letter. You can select many files by positioning the bar and pressing Enter, once for each file you want to select. When all the files are selected, you press the option letter and the option will function on only those that are selected.

In order to select various files, you need to match the bar to the various files. The "Home" key will adjust the display such that the first file is in the upper left–hand corner with the bar on it. The "End" key will adjust the display such that the last file is at the bottom right–hand corner with the bar on it. (If there are fewer than 26 files to display, all files will be displayed with the bar on the last.) Left arrow keys will move the bar back and forth between the Right and Left sides of the two column display.

The Up and Down arrow keys cause movement up and down one line at a time. The PgUp and PgDn keys will cause movement 7 lines at a time (half of a side). The movement will be either the bar moving itself or a scrolling of the files. The Scroll Lock key, when active, will hold the bar stationary and cause the files to scroll. When the Scroll Lock key is not active, the bar will move. The bar will always highlight a file. So, when Scroll Lock is active and the files cannot be scrolled due to a lack of files to list, the bar will move. Conversely, when Scroll Lock is inactive and the bar is at the beginning or end of the display, the files will be scrolled instead.

When PC Tools Deluxe is first executed, it uses the current setting at the Scroll Lock key. If Scroll Lock is active, the bar is positioned in the middle on the left side of a two–column display. When scrolling, this will allow you to visually scan ahead of the bar and to anticipate when to stop scrolling. If this is inconvenient, just press the Scroll Lock key to change the scrolling technique.

Selecting an Option

All PC Tools Deluxe options are listed in the bottom box of the PC Tools Deluxe "File Functions" menu. There are actually two command windows. One for "file" commands, one for "disk and special functions". You can switch between them by pressing the "F3" function key. The first window includes standard file oriented commands like Copy, Compare, Find, Rename, Delete, Verify, etc. The second command window lists disk and miscellaneous commands such as Copy and Compare disks, Locate and Undelete files, Add, Delete, and Rename subdirectories.

To begin, select the correct drive and subdirectory. If the drive/subdirectory presently displayed is not the one you wish, press "F10" to change either. (See "Selecting Drives" and "Selecting Subdirectories" which follow.) Note that a file in the directory is displayed in an inverse or colored field. By using the cursor keys, you can cause any file in the directory to be in the inverse or colored field. See "Scrolling the File Functions Display" for a complete explanation.

As before, if the directory is very large, you can also press F8 and select to limit which files you see. If the disk contains subdirectories, pressing F10 will return you to the subdirectory display.

On the File Functions menu, you need to indicate the files upon which to perform the function. There are three ways to accomplish this. First, if you will be performing the function on just one file, you need only move the inverse bar to the file and then press the appropriate highlighted key ("E" to view/Edit, for example).

Another method can be used if you will be performing the function on more than one file. To do this, you simply need to select the files. To select a file, move the inverse bar to it and press ENTER. You will note that a number will be placed to the left of the current (highlighted) file, and the inverse bar will automatically move down one line.

You will note that after a function is complete, any files you have selected, will remain so. This is for your convenience in performing subsequent functions on the same files. To unselect all files, just press F1.

You will also note that as files are selected and unselected a count of the number of files selected and their total size is dynamically updated on the screen.

Pressing Enter will place a number to the left of the current (highlighted) file. The first Enter will place the number 1, the second a number 2, etc. These numbers represent the order in which the files will be processed. If you accidentally press Enter to number a file you don't want to process, just press Enter again. The number will disappear. You can also reorder the files by typing a number for the highlighted file. The rest of the files will be re-numbered accordingly.

In addition, you can select one or more files by pressing F9, for the "File Selection Argument". This looks much like the F8 Directory List Argument option. You enter a filename and extension with optional wildcard characters. In this option, however, every file that matches is marked with a number and selected to be processed. This lets you select many similar files with one command. For example, you could select to process every .COM file by pressing F9 and entering the name of:

```
Name = [*          ]
Ext  = [COM]
```

When you've selected all the files that you want to process, press the appropriate key, as explained above.

PC Tools Deluxe

If you have selected multiple files to, for example, Copy, then you decide you need to look at one of the files in the middle of the list, you can do so without unselecting all the files first. PC Tools Deluxe will let you move the highlighted bar to the single file you wish to examine, then press ALT-<command>, in this case, the letter "E" for "Edit". The ALT-E command will edit the file underneath the highlighted bar and will ignore any selected files. When you are done examining this file, you can then press the "C" key (without holding the ALT key down) and the Copy command will operate on the previously selected and numbered files.

In other words, holding down the ALT key while pressing any command key will cause the command to only be executed on the file underneath the highlighted bar. It will ignore any selected files.

(**Note:** You can use the IBM's PrtSc (Print Screen) feature at any time when using PC Tools Deluxe. If you want a print-out of any PC Tools Deluxe screen display, make sure your printer is ready, then hold down the Shift key and press PrtSc. The contents of the screen will be printed. Any special graphics characters on the screen are converted into printable characters before being sent to the printer.)

The "F2" function key will switch between the standard, two-column directory list format (which shows 26 files at a time) to the expanded format. The expanded format displays only 13 files, but includes the time, number of clusters occupied by the file, and expands the file attribute codes into complete words. You may switch back and forth between the two types of lists at any time by pressing "F2".

If you have sub-directories on your disk, you can change the directory shown by PC Tools Deluxe by pressing the "F10" function key labeled "chg drive/path".

Selecting Drives

When you press the "F10" function key to change the drive/path displayed by PC Tools Deluxe, a box will appear on the center of the screen, similar to the following:

```
----------------------------------------
| Enter New Drive Letter below.  Press  |
| RTN for no change, "Esc" to return    |
|       New Drive ID  -  [A]            |
|     Valid letters are A thru B.       |
----------------------------------------
```

(If you have more than two drives, the valid letters will be different.)

This prompt lets you choose which drive you display the directory of. The drive that was used last appears in the brackets. If you want a directory of this drive, just press Enter. If you want a directory of another drive, type the letter for that drive, then press Enter.

Selecting Subdirectories

What happens next depends on whether or not the disk contains subdirectories. If it does, an additional display appears so that you can select which subdirectory you want.

The disk will whir for a few moments and the screen will display:

```
        Reading root directory...
```

then:

PC Tools Deluxe

Scanning sub-directories...

Then a new screen will appear:

```
PC Tools Deluxe - RX.xx                    Volume Label=PCTOOLS
----------------------Path Functions-------------------------
                                       BLINK=DOS CURRENT
Path=A:\

R---SUB1
O  |-SUB2---------SUBSUB1
O  |                |-SUBSUB2
T  |-SUB3
   |-SUB4




   Use cursor arrow keys to follow the tree to the desired directory
     Press ENTER to accept the choice. Press "Esc" to return
```

This diagram shows that the main, or "root", directory has four subdirectories, named SUB1, SUB2, SUB3, and SUB4. In addition, the subdirectory SUB2 contains two subdirectories of its own, called SUBSUB1 and SUBSUB2. (This is called a "tree" diagram because the subdirectories extend from the "root" directory like branches on a tree.)

By using the cursor and page up/down and/or Home/End keys on the numeric keypad, you can select any subdirectory. You can move up, down, right, or left, following the "branches" between directories.

When the directory you want is selected, press Enter to actually see the files in that directory.

Directory

After you've selected the subdirectory you want, or if the disk does not contain any subdirectories, the actual file display will appear next. (The following example is from the ROOT directory of the PC Tools Deluxe disk.)

```
PC Tools Deluxe RX.xx                                Vol Label=PC Tools
-------------------------File Functions----------------------Scroll Lock ON
Path=A: \*.*
Name    Ext    Size    Attr    Date    Name   Ext    Size    Attr    Date
IBMBIO  COM    12288   HSR.    1/01/80
IBMDOS  COM    12288   HSR.    1/01/80
PCTOOLS EXE    83840   ...A    9/14/85




+----------------------------------------------------------------------+
|3 files LISTed    =  108416 bytes.    3 files in sub-dir = 108416 bytes.|
| 0 files SELECTed =       0 bytes.    Available on volume =  68096 bytes.|
|----------------------------------------------------------------------|
| Copy Move cOmpare Find Rename Delete Verify view/Edit Attribute Print List |
| Sort Help RTN=selct F1=UNselect F2=alt dir 1st F3=other menu Esc=exit PCTls |
| F8=directory LIST argument F9=file SELECTion argument F10=change drive/path|
+----------------------------------------------------------------------+
```

In the upper right corner, the volume label is displayed if there is one. Each file in the directory is listed next, with the following information (depending on which directory list format you have chosen):

Name   The name of the file.

Ext   The extension name, if any.

Size   The number of bytes in the file.

#Clu   The number of disk "clusters" used by the file. This is a more accurate indication of how much disk space a file uses, since a file uses up disk space a cluster at a time. (This is only displayed on the expanded ALT–DIR display.)

Date   The date the file was last changed.

Time   The time of day the file was last changed. (This is only displayed on the expanded ALT–DIR display.)

Attributes Any "attributes" for the file.

Any IBM file can be marked with one or more "attributes". Most files will be marked as Normal and Archive, but there are a few exceptions. The possible attributes are:

Read–Only (abbreviated "R" on the two–column display) – If a file is marked as Read–Only, then the file can't be changed or erased by DOS. Read–Only provides a good way of protecting files from being accidentally erased.

Hidden ("H") – If a file is marked as Hidden, it does not appear in a normal DOS DIRectory.

System ("S") – Like Hidden, a file marked as System does not appear in a normal DOS DIRectory. (The two DOS system files IBMBIO.COM and IBMDOS.COM are marked as both Hidden and System, and are not listed when you type DIR from DOS.)

Normal – If a file is not marked as Read–Only, Hidden, or System, PC Tools Deluxe labels it as Normal. (Not explicitly shown on the two–column display.)

Archive ("A") – The Archive attribute is used by the DOS BACKUP program (and the PC Tools Deluxe PCBACKUP program) to decide which files to back up. Whenever DOS makes any change to a file, it marks it as Archive, which means the changed file should be backed up. When BACKUP backs up a file, it unmarks it again, meaning it has now been backed up.

(The Attribute option of PC Tools Deluxe, which is described later, provides a way for you to change the attributes or date and time of any file.)

There are a couple of other things to notice about the PC Tools Deluxe directory. 1) Unlike a DOS DIRectory, all Hidden and System files are listed. That way you can see exactly what files are on your disks, even if the files are marked as Hidden or System. 2) Subdirectory entries, however, do not appear with the other files in the PC Tools Deluxe directory. They are shown separately in the Subdirectory display (described earlier), so you can easily choose which directory or subdirectory you want to work with.

Directory PRINTING

You can print the disk directory at any time by typing "L" for "List". It will list all files in the selected directory, not just what is shown on the screen. (If you wish to list only the files on the screen, press shift–PrtSc.) You can sort (see below) the directory first to produce a more ordered directory list. You can restrict the files printed by using F8 to enter a Directory List Argument (see below). This will be reflected in the path information on line 3 of the display.

Directory SORTING

You can sort the disk directory by filename, extension, size, or date and time. Press "S" for "Sort". A new set of help lines will appear at the bottom of the screen:

```
Choose the sorting method desired.If it appears as desired,
      enter "U" to update the directory on the disk.
F7=by NAME F8=by EXT F9=by SIZE F10=by DATE/TIME ESC =return
```

When you press the appropriate function key, the directory (as stored in the computer's memory) is instantly sorted and the files are re–displayed in the new order. Sorts can be in ascending or descending order. If you want to make the changes permanent, press "U" to update the actual directory on the disk. Unless you update the directory by pressing "U", the sorted order will last only until you change directories in PC Tools Deluxe. The directory on the disk will remain unchanged. If you do not want to make changes permanent, just press ESC to work with the sorted list.

If considerable file creations and deletions have occurred, gaps may be present in the directory. These gaps will slow down any file searching that DOS will perform from time to time. Sorting your directories in any manner (and updating them by pressing "U") will remove these gaps. By so doing, you will increase the performance of your computer. Also, PC Tools Deluxe, while sorting, will move the subdirectory entries to the front regardless of the sorting technique. This will speed up DOS path searching.

Directory LIST Argument

Suppose, for example, that you want to see only those files which begin with the letter "I", or you want to see only the "COM" files. You can limit which files are displayed by pressing the F8 key.

When you press F8, you're presented with a new screen:

```
PC Tools Deluxe - RX.xx                 Volume Label=None
--------------------File Functions--------------------
Path=A:\

Enter the Directory List argument.

    Enter the name and/or extension to be used as a search
    argument for the directory listing. A question mark (?)
    is a "WILDCARD" which will always match any character
    found in that position. An asterisk (*) in the name or
    extension will match that position and all remaining
    positions.

            Name=[*      ]
            Ext =[*  ]

    Name and extension correct as entered, (Y/N)?  [y]


    F10 = Blank the Name and Extension. Esc = Return.
```

The screen instructions explain how you can use "?" and "*" to
match different filenames. The "wildcard" characters work just
like those used in DOS. Here are a few examples:

```
Name=[*    ]
Ext =[*    ]
```

will match all files and show the entire directory.

```
Name=[I*         ]
Ext =[*  ]
```

matches any file that begins with the letter "I".

```
Name=[*    ]
Ext =[COM]
```

matches only the files with an extension of "COM".

```
Name=[F?N        ]
Ext =[BAK]
```

will match the files FAN.BAK, FIN.BAK, FUN.BAK, or any filename with an F, any letter, an N, and an extension of BAK.

Type the name you want to match and press Enter, or just press Enter to accept the current name. Type in the extension in the same way. If you press the period key (.), it will automatically move from the filename to the extension line. If the name and extension have been changed to something else, you can press F10 to change them both back to "*". If you make a mistake, just answer the (Y/N) question with N for No, and you'll be able to retype them. Otherwise, press Y for Yes, and the directory will be re-displayed, showing only the files you selected. The currently selected directory list argument is shown on the path line of the directory display.

DIRECTORY MAINTENANCE

The Directory Maintenance option of PC Tools Deluxe allows you to Rename, Create, and Remove subdirectories. You can also change the current subdirectory for DOS and "prune and graft" sub–directories.

WARNING: If PC Tools Deluxe is resident, be sure that no files in the affected sub–directories are in use by another program. Also, remember to change any batch files, etc., that may depend on the old tree structure.

Directory Maintenance is located in the "Disk and Special Functions" menu (press "F3" from the "File Functions" menu). To begin, press the "D" key (for Directory maintenance). Next you will select the drive to work with as shown in the section "Selecting Drives". Once PC Tools Deluxe has read the directory information for the selected drives, you will see:

```
      Use Cursor arrow keys to follow the chain to the desired directory.
        Then choose a directory maintenance option below, or ESC to exit.
    F1=rename F2=create F3=remove F4=change DOS current directory F5=prune/graft
```

To rename, create or remove a sub–directory, or change the DOS current directory, simply choose the sub–directory and press the appropriate function key and follow the instructions displayed on the screen.

Prune and graft requires a bit of explanation. Let us assume you have three sub–directories as "branches" of the root directory. Let's call them TRUNK1, TRUNK2, and TRUNK3. Now, let's assume that TRUNK1 also has two "branches", called BRANCH1 and BRANCH2. And to make it interesting, assume BRANCH2 has a "branch", LIMB1. The tree display from PC Tools Deluxe will look something like this:

```
R
O--|--TRUNK1--|--BRANCH1
O  |           +--BRANCH2-----LIMB1
T  |--TRUNK2
   +--TRUNK3
```

Suppose you now want to change this structure, such that BRANCH2 (and LIMB1) are "branches" of TRUNK2. With the standard DOS utilities this would be a time–consuming and tedious task, indeed. But, with PC Tools Deluxe, it's easy!

Point to BRANCH2 using the cursor keys then press the "F5" function key to begin "Prune and Graft". Then confirm that this is the subdirectory you wish to prune by pressing the "P" key. Now, simply move to TRUNK2, using the cursor keys as usual and press Enter. You'll now be asked to confirm that you want to go ahead with the prune/graft operation. Indicate that you do and you'll get the revised tree display, looking something like this:

```
R
O--|--TRUNK1-----BRANCH1
O  |--TRUNK2-----BRANCH2-----LIMB1
T  +--TRUNK3
```

Once you have finished the desired task, pressing the ESC key will return you to the "Disk and Special Functions" screen shown.

COPY

Copy allows you to copy a group of files, or an entire disk.

COPY Files

The COPY FILES option allows you to copy normal DOS files quickly and easily.

You can copy the files:

1) from one disk to another, or
2) back onto the same disk with a different name, or
3) on the same disk into a different subdirectory (if the disk contains subdirectories).

To begin, select the correct drive, subdirectory and file(s) as described earlier in this chapter.

When you've selected all the files that you want to copy, press "C" for "Copy" to begin. PC Tools Deluxe will ask you for the Target drive as shown below. If only one drive is being used, you will be prompted to insert the proper disk when necessary.

```
==========================================
| Enter TARGET Drive ID - [B]            |
|                                        |
| Valid letters are A thru B.            |
| Press ESC key to return to main menu.  |
==========================================
```

The directory on the TARGET disk is read. If this disk contains subdirectories, another subdirectory tree diagram will appear. Use the arrow keys and Enter to select which subdirectory you want to copy the files into.

The files are then copied from the SOURCE disk to the TARGET disk. The file currently being copied is always displayed on the screen. If you wish to stop the copying, press ESC.

If you selected more than one file, each will be processed in turn. After all files have been processed (or if you pressed ESC), you are returned to the "File Functions" menu. Any file(s) selected will remain selected for your convenience.

COPY Disk

COPY DISK is a fast, reliable routine for copying standard DOS-formatted disks. (It does not copy copy-protected disks.) COPY DISK formats as it copies, so disks do not have to be formatted ahead of time. To copy a disk, simply select the COPY option from the "Disk and Special Functions" menu (Press "F3" from the "File Functions" menu), choose the SOURCE and TARGET drives, insert the disks, and press Enter. If you're copying using only one drive, PC Tools will tell you when to insert each disk. If you need to stop the copying before it has finished, just press ESC.

There are 40 tracks on a disk (except for 3 1/2 inch disks and AT high capacity disks which have 80 tracks), numbered from 0 to 39. As COPY DISK makes the copy, it first reads a number of tracks from the SOURCE disk into memory, then writes those tracks to the TARGET disk. It repeats this process until all tracks are copied. As it makes the copy, PC Tools keeps you informed of what is happening, using a copy-status display at the bottom of the screen. For double-sided 360K disks, it looks like this:

```
                     1         2         3         3
Track  0123456789012345678901234567890123456789
Side 0 .....RRRRRRRRRR
Side 1 ....WRRRRRRRRRR
```

After the word "Track" are the track numbers from 0 to 39. For every track read, an "R" is displayed. Then PC Tools shows an "F" when the track on the target disk is formatted, and a "W" as the track is written. After the track is copied successfully, a dot (.) appears. If an error is detected in the copy process an "E" will be shown instead of a dot (.). An "E" indicates an unsuccessful copy. The TARGET disk may be bad or the drive may need cleaning.

COPY DISK will take advantage of as much memory as it has access to. Therefore, if PC Tools Deluxe has been made memory resident, disk swaps may be required on single drive systems.

When the disk copy is finished, the main menu reappears.

MOVE

MOVE Files

Move operates exactly the same as Copy, except that the source file is deleted after the copy is successfully completed.

To begin, select the correct drive, subdirectory, and file(s) as described earlier in this chapter.

When you've selected all the files that you want to move, press "M" for "Move" to begin. You'll be asked to confirm that you really want to delete the source files. If so, after each file is copied, the source file will be deleted.

If you've selected more than one file, each will be processed in turn. After all files have been processed (or if you pressed ESC), you are returned to the "File Functions" menu.

Note: When moving files on a hard disk from one subdirectory to another, the files will not be physically moved. Only the directory entry is changed.

COMPARE

Compare will allow you to see if two different disks or files are identical.

COMPARE File

The COMPARE FILE option is similar to the DOS command COMP. It compares two files to see if they are identical. It can also compare several pairs of files at once.

As with the COPY FILES option, the files to be compared can be:

1) on different disks, with either the same filename or different filenames,
2) on the same disk in a different subdirectory, with either the same filename or different filenames, or
3) on the same disk and directory, with different filenames.

To begin, select the correct drive, subdirectory and file(s) as described earlier in this chapter.

After you've selected the files you want to compare, press "O" for "cOmpare" to begin the compare. You'll be prompted for the drive containing the files to be compared, then:

```
If you want to compare all files with
matching names, press "Y".
Otherwise, press any key to continue.
```

If you press "Y", PC Tools Deluxe will compare the files you selected with files of the same name on the SECOND drive. If you press any other key, PC Tools Deluxe will ask you (in a moment) for the filename you want to compare each selected file with.

Next, the SECOND drive whirs. If this disk contains subdirectories, another subdirectory "tree" display appears for you to select which subdirectory the files to be compared with are in.

Now the actual file comparing begins. If you answered "Y" to the matching files question, PC Tools Deluxe will look for those same names on the SECOND drive and compare the files. If you pressed any other key, then for each file you'll see a display similar to the following:

```
PC Tools Deluxe - RX.xx              Volume Label=None
----------------File Compare Service---------------
Path=A:\

TO Path=B:\

FILE1   .EXT is being compared

Please enter name and extension of file to compare
(ESC will end)


        Name=[FILE1   ]
        Ext =[EXT]
```

Note that it shows you what paths the files to be compared are on. If you want to compare with the same filename, just press Enter twice. Otherwise type in the new filename and extension. It will display:

```
FILE1 .EXT (on Drive A) is being COMPARED to FILE2 .EXT (on Drive B)
Enter "G" to proceed with compare
   or ESC to ignore
```

Press "G" to compare the two files. PC Tools Deluxe will read each file. If the files have different lengths, it will say so right away. If the contents of the two files differ at all, it will tell you which sector and which position in the sector the first difference was found in, and what those different values in each file are.

If you selected more than one file, each will be processed in turn. After all files have been processed (or if you pressed ESC), you are returned to the "File Functions" menu. Any file(s) selected will remain selected for your convenience.

COMPARE Disk

The COMPARE DISK option is similar to the DOS external command DISKCOMP. It compares two disks to see if they are identical. If there are any differences, it will show you what and where those differences are.

Compare disk is selected from the "Disk and Special Functions" menu (press "F3" from the "File Functions" menu). To start, type "O" for "cOmpare".

After you select which drives to use, PC Tools Deluxe will prompt you to insert the disks into the proper drives and press a key. It will then begin reading the disk in the first drive, then comparing it with the disk in the second drive. As it compares, a track status display (similar to the one used in COPY DISK) is shown at the bottom of the screen, similar to this:

```
              1         2         3         3
Track 012345678901234567890123456789012345678 9
Side 0 ....CRRRRRRRRRR
Side 1 ....RRRRRRRRRR
```

PC Tools Deluxe

PC Tools Deluxe displays an "R" for every track it reads. Then as the track is compared, a "C" replaces the "R". If the track compare is successful, a period replaces the "C".

If any differences are found, PC Tools Deluxe tells you the sector number and the offset within the sector of each difference, along with the two differing values. You can either press ESC to exit to the "Disk and Special Functions" menu, or press any other key to continue comparing.

If a disk error occurs, PC Tools Deluxe will tell you which logical sector was bad then display an "E" in the track status display for this track. This doesn't necessarily mean the entire track is bad, it just helps you remember which tracks had errors.

PC Tools

FIND

The FIND option lets you look for a byte or a string of bytes on the disk or within a file. You can enter the bytes as either hexadecimal values or text (ASCII) characters.

FIND File

To begin, select the correct drive, subdirectory, and file(s) as described earlier in this chapter.

When all of the files you want are selected, press "F" for "Find". The search string display will appear next:

```
PC Tools Deluxe - RX.xx                              Volume = None
--------------------------File Find Service---------------------------
Path = A:\
File = FILENAME.EXT

Please enter character string for which to scan below.
(You may enter the search string in ASCII or HEX. You may change entry modes by
pressing F1.)

[                                                        ]  <--ASCII
----------------------------------------------------------------
0 0 0 0 0 0 0 0 0 1 1 1 1 1 1 1 1 1 1 2 2 2 2 2 2 2 2 2 2 3 3 3
1 2 3 4 5 6 7 8 9 0 1 2 3 4 5 6 7 8 9 0 1 2 3 4 5 6 7 8 9 0 1 2
----------------------------------------------------------------
[                                                        ]  <--HEX

RTN=begin search  F1=toggle entry mode  ESC=exit
```

If you want to look for a string of text characters, just type the characters. The corresponding hexadecimal values will appear below. If you want to look for hex values, first press F1. The cursor will move down to the HEX line. Now type in the two-digit hex values. PC Tools Deluxe will check to see that you're entering valid hexadecimal numbers (digits 0 thru 9, A thru F). If you make a mistake, the speaker will beep.

When you're finished entering text characters or hex values, press Enter to begin the actual search. The disk will whir as PC Tools Deluxe reads each sector of the file or files, looking for the bytes you entered. (Note: The search is not "case–sensitive". In other words, you can enter text as any combination of uppercase and lowercase letters; PC Tools Deluxe will find any matching string, even if the case is different.) If it finds the string of bytes, it will display:

```
Search argument found in relative sector xxxx at offset xxx
Press "E" to view/edit the sector or
     "G" to continue searching.
```

To search for another occurrence of the same bytes, press "G" to continue the search.

If you want to view or edit the sector that contains the string, press "E" for Edit. The VIEW/EDIT display will appear for that sector, with the cursor on the first byte of the matching string. You can make changes to this sector if you like. (See the section on VIEW/EDIT later in the manual for a description of this display.) When you exit the VIEW/EDIT option, you're returned to the SEARCH screen so that you can continue the search with "G".

If the bytes cannot be found, or if you press ESC to stop the search, PC Tools Deluxe simply shows:

```
Search complete.
Press any key to continue.
```

If you selected more than one file, each will be processed in turn. After all files have been processed (or if you pressed ESC), you are returned to the "File Functions" menu. Any file(s) selected will remain selected for your convenience.

FIND Disk

The FIND by DISK option is very similar to FIND by FILE. You enter a string of bytes to search for, as either text characters or hexadecimal values. If PC Tools Deluxe finds the bytes anywhere on the disk, it will tell you on what sector they were found and give you the file name they were found in.

After you've selected the FIND by DISK option from the "Disk and Special Functions" menu (press the "F3" key from the "File Functions" menu) and chosen an appropriate drive, a search string display will appear, similar to the one used in FIND by FILE. (See FIND FILE, described earlier.) Enter the bytes you want to search for. You can enter them on the top line as text characters, or press F1 and enter them on the bottom line as hexadecimal values. When you've typed in the bytes you want to search for, press Enter.

The disk will whir as PC Tools Deluxe looks for the bytes. If it finds them, it will display:

```
Search argument found in relative sector nnnnn at offset xxx
Press "E" to view/edit the sector or
    "G" to continue searching.
```

(Note that the sector number shown here is the absolute sector number on the disk. In SEARCH by FILE, however, the relative sector number in the file is shown instead of the number of sectors from the beginning of the disk.)

To view or edit that sector on the disk, press "E" for Edit. To search for another occurrence of the same string of bytes, press "G". To exit, press ESC.

RENAME

Rename will allow you to rename files or the disk volume label.

RENAME File

You can change the name of one or more files using the RENAME FILE option.

To begin, select the correct drive, subdirectory, and file(s) as described earlier in this chapter.

When the files you want to rename are selected, press "R" for "Rename". For each file you selected, the following will be displayed:

```
PC Tools Deluxe - RX.xx                              Volume=None
----------------------------File Rename Service---------------------
Path=B:\


FILENAME.EXT is being renamed

Please enter the new file and extension names
(ESC will end)


        Name=[FILENAME]
        Ext =[EXT]
```

Type in the new filename. If you only need to change one or two letters of the filename, you can use the right and left arrow keys to position the cursor where you want, then type in the new letters. If you're renaming to a shorter filename, you'll need to type spaces to clear out the rest of the old name. Press Enter.

After you've entered the new name, you'll see:

```
FILENAME.EXT is to be RENAMED to NEWNAME .NEW

Please confirm. "Y" to RENAME
               "N" to REENTER
               "B" to BYPASS
               ESC to RETURN
```

Press "Y" for Yes to rename the file. The disk will whir as the name change is made permanent. Press "N" for No if you made a mistake entering the new filename. You'll get another chance to enter the new name. Press "B" for Bypass to skip this file (without renaming it). Press ESC to exit if you don't want to rename any more of the selected files.

If you selected more than one file, each will be processed in turn. After all files have been processed (or if you pressed ESC), you are returned to the "File Functions" menu. Any file(s) selected will remain selected for your convenience.

RENAME Disk

The RENAME DISK option allows you to rename, add or remove a volume label to your diskettes. Select this option from the "Disk and Special Functions" menu (press the "F3" key from the "File Functions" menu) by typing "R" for "Rename". Then it asks for a drive letter. Then displays:

```
PC Tools Deluxe - RX.xx
--------------Disk Rename Service---------------

Drive B

Current volume label=OLDLABEL

Enter the new volume label      [               ]

ESC to return to main menu
```

Type in the the new volume label name and press Enter. The disk will whir as the volumn is renamed. (Press ESC if you decide you don't want to rename the volume label.) If you blank the name, the volume label will be removed.

DELETE

The DELETE option lets you delete (or "Erase") one or more files from a disk. To begin, select the correct drive, subdirectory, and file(s) as described earlier in this chapter.

When the files are selected, press "D" for "Delete".

If you've selected more than one file, you'll see:

```
You have selected multiple files to delete.

If you want to delete all files without
individual confirmations, press "Y".
For individual confirmations, press "N".

Press ESC to Exit
```

If you're sure that you want to delete all the files you've selected, press "Y". The disk will whir as those files are deleted.

If you want to double–check each file before it is deleted, or if you selected only one file to delete, you'll see for each file:

```
FILENAME.EXT is to be DELETED

Please confirm. "Y" to DELETE
               "N" to bypass

         Press ESC to Exit
```

Press "Y" to delete this file. Press "N" if you don't want to delete the file. Then the next file to be deleted will be displayed.

If you selected more than one file, each will be processed in turn. After all files have been processed (or if you pressed ESC), you are returned to the "File Functions" menu. Any file(s) selected will remain selected for your convenience.

VERIFY

Verify allows you to confirm that there are no bad spots in any of your files or on any of your disks.

VERIFY File

The VERIFY FILE option reads all of the sectors in a file to make certain the entire file can be read without any disk errors. To begin, select the correct drive, subdirectory, and file(s) as described earlier.

When the files you want to verify are selected, press "V" for "Verify".

For each file you'll see:

```
FILENAME.EXT is being verified.   Reading sector xxxxx
```

The sector number shown will change rapidly as PC Tools Deluxe reads each sector of the file. If there are no errors while reading the file, PC Tools Deluxe displays:

```
FILENAME.EXT verifies OK!
```

and the next file in turn is verified. If there is an error, PC Tools Deluxe will display:

```
FILENAME.EXT has an ERROR in logical sector xxxxxxx
```

If you selected more than one file, each will be processed in turn. After all files have been processed (or if you pressed ESC), you are returned to the "File Functions" menu. Any file(s) selected will remain selected for your convenience.

If an error is found PC Tools Deluxe will allow you to run View/Edit on that sector to attempt to repair the data.

VERIFY Disk

This option lets you verify that all of the information on your DOS disk is readable, including files, subdirectories, and volume information. VERIFY DISK is designed to work with formatted DOS disks which are not copy-protected. (It does not work with blank unformatted disks because a blank disk does not contain any information to verify.)

Select this option from the "Disk and Special Functions" menu (press "F3" key from the "File Functions" menu) by typing "V" for "Verify". After entering the drive letter, PC Tools Deluxe will display:

```
Drive B is about to be verified,
  Press any key to continue
      Press ESC to Exit
```

To proceed with the verify, press a key. PC Tools Deluxe will read the sectors of the disk, checking for disk errors:

```
Drive B is being verified.
Currently reading logical sectors xxxxxxx thru yyyyyyy.
```

If a bad sector not previously marked bad by PC Tools or DOS occurs on any sector, you will be shown the number of the sector in error. You will be told if the sector is part of the DOS system area, part of an existing file or available for use. If the sector is available, PC Tools Deluxe will optionally mark the sector as bad to prevent future use. If it is already allocated to a file or subdirectory, it will recommend that you run the "Surface Scan" option of Compress to move the file data. In any case, you can use View/Edit DISK to attempt correction of the problem.

You can press ESC to return to the "Disk and Special Functions" menu, or press any other key to continue verifying the rest of the disk.

WORD PROCESSOR

PC Tools Deluxe includes a limited Word Processor (or text editor) that allows you to create or edit documents, even within other running programs. Unlike the View/Edit option of PC Tools Deluxe, the Word Processor will allow you to create new files and change existing ones using a format that is common to most popular word processing programs. You can even print your documents with Page numbers; set left, right, top, and bottom margins; and enter page headings and footings with the Print command – all without leaving PC Tools Deluxe.

Unlike many word processors, the PC Tools Deluxe word processor will only keep a limited section of the file you are editing in memory at a time – the rest is stored in a temporary "spillfile" on the disk. This allows you to edit large documents even in resident mode without preallocating extra memory to PC Tools Deluxe.

Getting Started

The Word Processor is started by typing "W" from the file display. If you want to edit an existing file, position the highlighted bar over the file to be edited. Then press "W". If you want to create a new file, just press the "W" key – it doesn't matter where the highlighted bar is.

PC Tools Deluxe will next confirm that you wish to edit this file. The reason it does this is that it still thinks you might wish to create a new file. If you want to load the file you selected earlier, press any key. To create a new file, press the "F2" function key, and you will be ready to create a new document.

Moving Around

The Word Processor is very easy to use. The arrow and page up/down keys will move you around in the file. The Home key will take you first to the beginning of the current line, then subsequent presses will move you to the top left of the screen. The End key will move the cursor to the end of the line, the lower left of the screen if pressed again. Holding down the CTRL key at the same time as pressing the Home key will move you to the beginning of the document, and holding down the CTRL key at the same time as pressing the End key will move you to the end of the document.

Adding and Editing Text

To add text, just type – the word processor will automatically wrap words around on the screen for you. The only time you need to press the "return" key is to end a paragraph. If you want to edit existing text, use the editing keys described above to position the cursor over the text to edit. Then either type new text to add here or press the DEL key to delete characters starting here.

The Word Processor normally comes up in "Insert" mode. This means any new text typed will be inserted into the document. If you are editing, and want the new text to overtype existing text, press the INS (insert) key first. The insert key "toggles" the Word Processor between insert and overtype modes. When the "INS" indicator is shown on the bottom of the screen, you are in insert mode.

The TAB key works just like the Tab key on a typewriter: it will move the cursor to the next tab position on the page. Tabs are pre-set in the PC Tools word processor to every ninth position across the screen. They are very helpful in lining up columns of information.

Eight of the function keys have a special meaning to the word processor. They are:

Function Key F2 = SAVE the current document
Function Key F3 = SEARCH for text in the document
Function Key F4 = SEARCH then REPLACE text in the
                   document
Function Key F5 = SELECT a block of text (used with F6 &
                   F7 keys)
Function Key F6 = CUT (delete) the selected text and put it
                   into the PASTE buffer
Function Key F7 = COPY (move) a copy of the selected text
                   into the PASTE buffer.
Function Key F8 = PASTE (insert) a CUT or COPIED block of
                   text at the cursor
Function Key F10 = Shows carriage returns in the file. Normally
                   they are not displayed.

And finally, the ESC key will exit the word processor. If you have
made any changes, it will not let you exit without confirming that
you don't want to save your work. This is to prevent you from
accidentally pressing ESC and losing the document.

Cutting and Pasting Text

The word processor has four Function Keys that help you work
with blocks of text. They are F5 (SELECT), F6 (CUT), F7
(COPY), and F8 (PASTE). Here's how they work:

The F5 (SELECT) command will put the word processor into
"select" mode. In this mode, when you move through your
document with the cursor keys, the text will be "highlighted". It
will always start highlighting text from the cursor position when
you pressed the F5 key. For example, to select a paragraph, you
can move to the beginning or end of the paragraph and press
"F5". Next, use the arrow keys to move into the paragraph. Each
time you press the up or down arrow key, another line is
highlighted (selected). Each time you press the left or right arrow
key another character is selected. If you press the Page up or
Page down keys, a page of text will be selected.

If you want to "undo" selected text, press F5 again and it will exit SELECT mode.

When you have selected all the text you want to delete or move somewhere else, press the F6 (CUT) function key. The Cut command will delete all the text you have selected and will put it into the invisible PASTE buffer so you can insert (PASTE) it somewhere else in your document.

If you want to leave the selected text where it is, but you want to make a copy of it to put somewhere else in your document, press the F7 (COPY) key instead of F6 (CUT). COPY works just like CUT except the selected text is not deleted: it is only copied into the paste buffer.

Now that the PASTE buffer contains the text you have SELECTED, then CUT or COPIED, use the cursor keys to move to where you would like to insert the text. Notice that pressing the CUT or COPY keys automatically takes you out of SELECT mode.

When the cursor is at the point to insert the next, just press the F8 (PASTE) key and the text will appear.

Note: The PASTE buffer will only hold the last CUT or COPIED text. If you want to move two different sections of your document, you will need to move them one at a time. Pressing the CUT or COPY keys will remove any existing text in the PASTE buffer and insert the next text.

Saving Text

You can save your work as you type by pressing the F2 Function Key. When you are ready to exit the Word Processor, you can just press ESC and PC Tools will confirm that you want to save before leaving. Everytime you save, PC Tools will rename the previous version of your document to name.BAK, so if you ever want to undo your work, you can edit your old file.

Printing

PC Tools Deluxe has new formatted printing capabilities using the "P" (Print) command. To print your text, exit out of the word processor with ESC after saving your document, move the highlighted bar to the file you wish to print, and press the P key to invoke the Print options.

For more information on formatted printing, please refer to the PC Tools Deluxe Print command.

VIEW/EDIT

The VIEW/EDIT option allows you to view the contents of any sector of a file, or any sector on the disk, and makes changes to the sector if you want. It can also be used to fix some kinds of disk errors. A good understanding of hexadecimal, bytes, and ASCII is helpful when using VIEW/EDIT.

VIEW/EDIT File

To begin, select the correct drive, subdirectory, and file(s) as described earlier in this chapter. When the files you want to VIEW/EDIT are selected, press "E" for View/Edit. (See View/Edit continued below.)

VIEW/EDIT Disk

To look at any sector on the disk (whether or not it is part of a file), select "E" for "View/Edit" from the "Disk and Special Functions" menu (press "F3" from the main PC Tools Deluxe menu). Choose an appropriate drive letter. The disk will whir as PC Tools Deluxe reads the first sector (sector 0) from the disk.

VIEW/EDIT (Continued)

The VIEW/EDIT displays for FILE and DISK are very similar. You'll see something like this:

```
PC Tools Deluxe - RX.xx                          Volume Label = None
---------------------------Disk View/Edit Service---------------------------
Path=B:\*.*
                    Relative sector being displayed is: xxxxxxxx


Displacement    --------------------Hex codes------------------  ASCII value

 0000 (0000)    50 43 54 4F 4F 4C 53 20 45 58 45 20 00 00 00 00  PCTOOLS EXE

 0016 (0010)    00 00 00 00 00 00 70 5A D9 0A AB 00 00 32 01 00      pZ+

 0032 (0020)    50 48 4F 4E 45 20 20 20 20 20 20 10 00 00 00 00  PHONE    >

 0048 (0030)    00 00 00 00 00 00 7D 41 8C 07 E2 00 00 00 00 00      }A

 0064 (0040)    4E 4F 4B 45 59 20 20 20 44 4F 43 20 00 00 00 00  NOKEY DOC

 0080 (0050)    00 00 00 00 00 00 02 31 A1 0A D1 00 B7 15 00 00      1

 0096 (0060)    43 4F 50 59 49 49 50 43 45 58 45 20 00 00 00 00  COPYIIPCEXE

 0112 (0070)    00 00 00 00 00 00 67 49 8C 0A 60 02 80 7B 00 00    gI   . {

 0128 (0080)    4A 49 4D 20 20 20 20 20 20 20 20 20 00 00 00 00  JIM

 0144 (0090)    00 00 00 00 00 00 5C 7E 9D 0A 68 02 8E 01 00 00         ~  h

 0160 (00A0)    49 42 4D 33 36 20 20 20 20 20 20 10 00 00 00 00  IBM36    >

 0176 (00B0)    00 00 00 00 00 00 D1 80 A4 0A 17 03 00 00 00 00

 0192 (00C0)    E5 55 54 4F 45 58 45 43 42 41 54 20 00 00 00 00  AUTOEXECBAT

 0208 (00D0)    00 00 00 00 00 00 12 00 21 00 20 04 0E 00 00 00      .

 0224 (00E0)    E5 48 55 52 53 44 41 59 20 20 20 20 00 00 00 00  THURSDAY

 0240 (00F0)    00 00 00 00 00 00 87 06 EC 08 CC 00 A5 00 00 00


Home=beg of file/disk    End=end of file/disk

Esc=Exit  PgDn=forward  PgUp=back  F1=toggle mode  F2=chg sector num  F3=edit
```

Sectors on an IBM floppy disk contain 512 separate values, or bytes. On a hard disk, the sector size is usually a multiple of 512 but may vary from drive to drive. The VIEW/EDIT option shows 256 bytes, or half a sector, on the screen at a time.

Each line of the display shows 16 bytes from the sector, displayed as two-digit hexadecimal numbers in the middle area, then the same 16 values as ASCII characters on the right. Some or all of the characters may appear as gibberish. This is because those bytes may be program or data values and were never intended to be displayed as text.

For the purposes of explanation, the following paragraphs assume a 512K byte sector size, but other sizes are correctly handled.

The numbers on the left are "offset " or "displacement " numbers. Think of the 512 bytes as being numbered from 0 as the first byte of the sector to 511 as the last byte (0000 to 01FF in hexadecimal). The first line shows the first 16 bytes, bytes 0 through 15. The next line shows the next 16 bytes, bytes 16 through 31; the next shows bytes 32 through 47, etc. The displacement number on the left tells you how many bytes into the sector each line is (0000, 0016, 0032, etc.) For example, the first byte on the first line is byte 0000; the first byte on the second line is byte 0016, etc. The numbers in parentheses are the same offset numbers in hexadecimal.

Notice the help lines at the bottom of the screen. Pressing the Page down (Pg Dn) key will show you the next half-sector. Pressing the Page down key repeatedly will move you through the file or disk a half-sector at a time (until you reach the end of the file or disk). The Page up (Pg Up) key moves you back to the previous half-sector. Home moves you to the first sector (sector 0), and End moves you to the last sector.

If you want to edit a certain cluster, press F2, then press "c" and enter the desired cluster number. If the cluster number you entered is too large for the file or disk you're viewing, PC Tools Deluxe will simply read the largest-numbered cluster it can. You can also specify certain areas of the disk to edit by name instead of cluster. After pressing F2, type:

"B"   to edit the BOOT sector
"F"   to edit the FAT sector
"R"   to edit the ROOT Directory sector
"D"   to edit the first DATA sector

If you are using VIEW/EDIT by file, you can see just the ASCII text without the hexadecimal values by pressing F1. Press F1 again to switch back to the mixed hex/ASCII display.

If you want to edit the sector (make changes to it), press F3. A blinking box cursor will appear over the first hex byte, and the help lines at the bottom of the screen will change to:

```
^ v > < = cursor F1=swap entry area F5=update F6=cancel update ESC=Exit
Home=first pos   End=last pos   PgUp=1st half   PgDn=2nd half
```

The four arrow keys will move the cursor from byte to byte. Place the cursor over the first byte you want to change. If you then type hexadecimal values, they will replace the old bytes at the cursor position. The new values will appear in color (or highlighted) so you can easily see the changes you've made.

If you want to enter new values as text characters instead of hex bytes, press F1. The cursor will move to the corresponding position in the ASCII character area on the right. Now any characters you type will replace the old characters. The new characters will appear in color (or highlighted) so you can see the changes. Press F1 again if you want to move the cursor back to the hex value area.

Press F5 to update the sector on the disk with the changes you've made. PC Tools Deluxe will write the changed sector to the disk. Press F6 if you want to cancel the update (not make any changes). PC Tools Deluxe will re-read the old sector from the disk again.

You can also press F4 to have View/Edit Disk tell you the name of the file any cluster belongs to. Once you press F4, it may take a few moments to find the name as it has to search all your directories and work backwards through the FAT.

Note: With the VIEW/EDIT option, you can often fix bad sectors. If you ask VIEW/EDIT to read a sector that contains an error, it will try to read the sector anyway. If it can succeed, the sector data will appear, along with the message "I/O error" near the top of the screen. If you want to fix this sector, press F3 for Edit, then F5 to update the sector. This will rewrite the same sector information back to the disk, this time without a disk error! (This makes the sector readable, but the information contained in the sector might still be incorrect.)

Press ESC to exit the VIEW/EDIT option.

UNDELETE

The UNDELETE option is designed to help you recover files which have been accidentally deleted or erased. It can also be used to restore deleted subdirectories, and the files they contained.

The Two Kinds of Undelete

PC Tools Deluxe can use two different approaches to recovering accidentally erased files. The standard approach assumes you have not installed the "Delete Tracking" option of the MIRROR program (described in its own chapter later in this manual). The disadvantages of the standard method are:

1. It cannot always fully recover "fragmented" files
2. The first letter of the file name will be lost

The "Delete Tracking" method does not have these limitations. It works by installing a small resident program each time you turn on your computer. Whenever DOS deletes a file, the resident program saves the deleted file's information in a special file called "PCTRACKR.DEL" in the Root Directory of your hard disk. (If your hard disk is partitioned, the "PCTRACKR.DEL" will reside in the Root Directory of the first partition. All partitions that were specified during start–up will be monitored from there.) Later, if you decide you want to undelete this file, PC Tools can recover the full file name and all its data, even if it is fragmented over your hard disk, provided the data has not been overwritten.

Therefore, we highly recommend that you use the "Delete Tracking" option of our MIRROR program. If you used PCSETUP with our recommended options to install PC Tools on your hard disk, then it has already been done for you.

How UNDELETE Works

When DOS "erases" a file, it does not actually obliterate all of the file information. It destroys the first letter of the filename in the file's directory entry, to mark this as an "erased" file. (Other information, such as the file's size and date, is still intact.) It also marks all of the sectors that the file had used as "free", so that the sectors can be used for something else. This process wipes out the record of which sectors the file had used. In other words, the file information is still on the disk, but there is no longer any record of WHERE on the disk it is, except for the first cluster. If the "Delete Tracking" option of MIRROR is installed, this information will be saved so PC Tools can recover it later. If it is not installed, you will have to supply the first letter of the file name and PC Tools will make its "best guess" as to where to find the file data. If the disk was fragmented, it might not be able to fully recover the file.

Remember: If you save or change any files on the disk after you've erased a file, you might not be able to recover the file.

Once a file is deleted, the disk space used by the deleted file is now available for other files. If you later change or save any new files on the disk, this could overwrite some or all of the deleted file's information, making it impossible to completely undelete the file. For this reason, if you accidentally delete a file, you should always use UNDELETE right away to recover the file before any information is lost. This is true whether you are using the "Delete Tracking" option or not.

Recommendation: On diskettes we suggest that you always copy the disk containing the file you wish to undelete and undelete the file on the copy. (You must use a disk copy program as opposed to a file copy program as file oriented copy programs cannot copy deleted files.) By doing this, you cannot inadvertently damage your only copy of an important data disk. Once the undelete has been successfully completed on the backup disk, you can copy the undeleted file from the backup disk to the original. (Obviously this cannot be done if your file is stored on a hard disk.)

Undelete Files

The Undelete Option of PC Tools Deluxe looks almost the same whether your are using the "Delete Tracking" option or not. If PC Tools Deluxe finds the special file that contains the deleted files information, it will ask you if you want to use it. If it does not find this file, the standard method will be used.

Suppose you've just deleted two files, named MYFILE1.DAT and MYFILE2.BAK, from a disk. To recover them, start up PC Tools Deluxe, press "F3" to get to the "Disk and Special Functions" menu and type "U" for "Undelete". A display similar to the usual "File Functions" menu will appear next:

```
    PC Tools Deluxe - RX.xx                   Volume Label=None
    ----------------File Undelete Service-----------Scroll Lock ON
    Path=B:\*.*
    Name     Ext     Size   #Clu     Date      Time    Attributes
    ?YFILE1  DAT@    6129     12    1/01/81    12:00p   Normal
    ?YFILE2  BAK@     700      2    6/22/83     4:36p   Normal




         @ = Automatic Recovery Possible

    Select file(s) to be un-deleted and then press "G" to proceed
  F8=drcty LIST argumnt F9=file SELECTion argumnt F10=chg drive/path
      ^v=scroll   <+=SELECT  F1=UNselect  F2=alt dir 1st  ESC=exit
```

Notice that the deleted files are displayed here, rather than active files as in most PC Tools Deluxe displays. If you do not have the "Delete Tracking" option of MIRROR installed, the first character of each filename was lost when the file was deleted so it appears as a question mark.

Note: If the display instead reads:

```
No Entries Found
```

then there aren't any deleted file entries in this subdirectory. Either you are not looking in the right subdirectory, no files were ever deleted, or else the deleted file entries were completely overwritten because new files have been saved on the disk. If you are not in the correct subdirectory, use the F10 function key to choose the subdirectory containing the deleted files.

The "@" character next to the file name tells you whether PC Tools thinks it can automatically undelete the file for you or not. If you are using the "Delete Tracking" method, this means that none of the file's clusters are currently being used by any other files. If you are using the standard undelete method, it means that the first part (first cluster) of the file is not being used by any other file.

If you see an "*" instead of an "@", and you are using the "Delete Tracking" method, it means that some clusters were available. If you see neither an "*" or an "@", then recovery is not possible as none were available. The "*" character indicates that the file has been partially or completely overwritten by another file.

When using the "Delete Tracking" method, you cannot undelete files that do not have the "@" next to the file name as the file has definitely been overwritten by another file. In other words, it is too late to completely recover this file. If you want to try to recover some of the data, you can press the ESC key to get back to the disk and special functions menu of PC Tools Deluxe and restart Undelete, this time saying "N" to the prompt asking if you wish to use the "Delete Tracking" method.

To Undelete a file or files, select them from the list of files shown using the cursor and Return keys as described earlier in this manual.

If you have the "Delete Tracking" option installed, that's all there is to it! PC Tools Deluxe will look in its special file, get the first letter of the file name and undelete the file for you automatically. You can ignore the rest of this chapter.

If you don't have the "Delete Tracking" option installed, you will need to tell PC Tools what the first letter of the file name is for each file you wish to undelete:

```
Enter first character-?YFILE1 .DAT
```

Type the correct first letter for the filename, and press Enter. (In this example, you would type the letter "M" and press Enter.)

If there's already an active file with that name, you'll see: "File already exists, press any key to continue". After pressing a key, you can either enter a different first character, or press ESC to exit.

Another display will appear:

PC Tools Deluxe

```
PC Tools Deluxe - RX.xx            Volume label=None
-------File Undelete Service--------Scroll Lock ON
Path=B:\
Name      Ext  Size  #Clu  Date    Time   Attributes
MYFILE    DAT  6129   12  1/01/81  12:00p Normal
------------------------------------------------



     Use function keys to make selection
     F1 - Automatic selection of clusters
     F2 - Manual selection of clusters
     ESC - Exit
```

PC Tools Deluxe knows where on the disk the first cluster of the file is, and can make intelligent, educated guesses as to where the subsequent clusters are. If you select F1, PC Tools Deluxe will attempt to recover the deleted file for you. If automatic file recovery is possible, an "@" will be displayed next to the file name. If it is not, you will have to manually select each sector. If you select automatic undeletion, the disk will whir for a few seconds as PC Tools Deluxe undeletes the file. You should then see the message:

```
File was successfully Undeleted - Press any key to continue
```

If you instead select F2, you can manually select which clusters you want to include in the recovered file. This option might be needed if the file, before it was deleted, had changed in size (for example, a word processor document that had been updated several times) and other files had been saved or deleted.

When you select F2, you'll see a display similar to the VIEW/EDIT display. PC Tools Deluxe presents to you, in order, the sectors that most likely belong to this file.

```
PC Tools Deluxe - RX.xx                          Volume Label = None
--------------------------File Undelete Service---------------------
Path=B:\
      Name       Ext    Size      #Clu               Time    Attributes
      IBMDOS     COM    27760       28     4/22/85   12:09p    Normal
====================================================================
|Cluster|                Data Display Area                          |
|number |                                                           |
  0124
Displacement --------------------Hex codes------------------ ASCII value
0000 (0000)   E9 FE 68 00 00 00 42 55 47 20 00 00 00 00 00 00   h  BUG
0016 (0010)   00 00 00 00 FF FF FF FF C3 13 03 00 01 00 FF FF       |
0032 (0020)   FF FF 00 00 00 00 00 00 00 00 00 98 00 00 00 00
0048 (0030)   00 00 00 00 00 00 80 00 00 00 00 00 00 00 00 00
0064 (0040)   00 00 00 00 00 00 00 00 00 00 00 00 04 80 18 14
0080 (0050)   1E 14 4E 55 4C 20 20 20 20 20 00 90 A5 15 00 00   ^ NUL
0096 (0060)   A9 15 00 00 A9 15 00 00 A5 15 00 00 A5 15 00 00
0112 (0070)   A5 15 00 00 A5 15 00 00 A5 15 00 00 A9 15 00 00
0128 (0080)   A5 15 00 00 A5 15 00 00 A5 15 00 00 A9 15 00 00
0144 (0090)   A5 15 00 00 A5 15 00 00 FF FF FF FF 05 00 00 00

                 0 out of  28 cluster(s)  added to the file

                  Home    End    PgUp    PgDn    Esc=Esc
         F1=Add to file and display next cluster   F2=Skip to next cluster
            F3=Save file   F4=Unselect   F5=Search   F6=Select cluster num
```

Notice that in this example, the directory entry says that this file contains 28 clusters. That means you will need to select 28 clusters to completely recover this file.

If the displayed cluster appears to be part of the deleted file, press F1. This will add the cluster to the file being recovered, then show you the next cluster to consider. If you don't want to add the current cluster to the file, press F2. The next cluster will be displayed with–out any other action. If the menu indicated automatic recovery was possible, (an "@" next to the file name), the first cluster PC Tools Deluxe displays is the one it knows to be the first cluster of the file. You should always press F1 to add this first cluster to the file.

If you accidentally add a cluster to the file then determine it wasn't the right one, you can remove it and display the previously selected cluster by pressing the F4 function key.

If your hard disk was fragmented, the next cluster PC Tools Deluxe picks for you might not be the right one. If you are trying to undelete a text file, you might be able to find the next cluster using the Search command. For example, looking at the text at the bottom of the current cluster using the cursor movement keys, you might see the beginning of a sentence "If your hard disk was frag". Using the F1 key would add this to the file and display the next cluster. If the next cluster doesn't start with the characters "mented" (the rest of the word "fragmented"), you would know this couldn't be the right cluster. So instead of pressing the F1 key again to add this incorrect cluster, you press the F5 key to search for the proper text on the hard disk. When it is found, you can continue adding clusters using the F1 key until the file is completely recovered.

In other words, if the file is fragmented on your hard disk, Undelete can be a more time–consuming, manual task. For this reason, especially if you aren't using the "Delete Tracking" option of MIRROR, we recommend that you run COMPRESS often.

When you think you've selected all of the clusters that belong to the file, press F3. This will rebuild and save the file using the clusters you've selected. To exit without changing the deleted file at all, press ESC. If you watch the count at the bottom, PC Tools Deluxe will, when the total cluster count is reached, automatically save the file.

After you've undeleted a file, you should try using the file to see if the Undelete was successful. If the wrong clusters were selected, the file will not contain all the same information as before it was deleted. If you have problems with an undeleted file, you can delete it and try to undelete it again, choosing different clusters this time.

When using either automatic or manual selection of clusters, you might get the message:

```
Cluster chain in use - Unable to recover this file
Press any key to continue
```

This means that another file was saved after this file was deleted, and it overwrote the first cluster of this file. The file can't be recovered, since the information is lost.

UNDELETE Subdirectories

It is possible to undelete subdirectories as well as files with PC Tools Deluxe. This is necessary if you delete all the files in a subdirectory, then delete the subdirectory. If you later wish to recover a file in the deleted subdirectory, you will first need to undelete the subdirectory itself.

Undeleting subdirectories works just like undeleting files, except that you will select "Sub-Dir" instead of "File" after selecting the "UNDELETE" option from the "Disk and Special Functions" menu of PC Tools Deluxe. Once you have successfully undeleted a subdirectory, you can then undelete its files as described earlier.

Changing File ATTRIBUTES

WARNING: You should not change the attributes of **copy-protected** files and **system** files. Changing these attributes can result in programs not running or your hard disk not booting!

Earlier in this manual (in the section entitled THE FILE DIRECTORY), file attributes were described. To summarize: The possible attributes a file can have are Read Only, Hidden, System, and Archive. The Read Only attribute prevents DOS from being able to change the contents of a file or deleting it. The Hidden and System attributes make a file "invisible" so that it is not listed when you enter the DOS DIR command. The Archive bit is used to tell the DOS program BACKUP which files have been updated since the last backup.

Using the ATTRIBUTE option of PC Tools Deluxe, you can change the attributes, and the date and time, of any file. Select the files to be processed and then press "A" for "Attribute". You'll see:

```
PC Tools Deluxe - RX.xx                          Volume=None
-------------------File Attribute Service--------------------
Path=B:\

File=FILENAME.EXT                           Size= 9564 bytes
                                            #Clu=    3 clusters

     Initial attributes shown indicate those in effect. To
     change attributes, use the arrows (^v) to select an
     attribute to change. ENTER (<-') will change (toggle)
     that attribute. Press "U" to Update and make the changes
     permanent. "ESC" will return without any change.

     Initial Attributes      New Attributes
     Read Only - OFF          Read Only - OFF
     Hidden    - OFF          Hidden    - OFF
     System    - OFF          System    - OFF
     Archive   - ON           Archive   - ON

     Initial Time/Date        New Time/Date
     12:01p                   12:01p
     11/20/84                 11/20/84

"U" to Update and make changes permanent. ESC to return without
 changes.
                 <-- = prior entry   --> = next entry
```

In the left column, the initial or current attributes and time/date for the file are shown. Notice the color (inverse) bar over the first attribute in the right column. Using the up and down arrow keys, you can move the bar to any attribute. Pressing the Enter key will 'toggle' the selected attribute from OFF to ON, or from ON to OFF.

If you want to change the date or the time of the file, press the down arrow key until a blinking cursor appears under the time or date line. Now type in a new time or a new date. Just type the digits, not the colon or the slashes. If you're entering a time with an hour of 9 or less (for example, 3:25), type a zero ahead of the digit (as in 03:25). (Don't forget to type either an "A" or "P" for AM and PM.) Similarly, if the date has a single–digit month (2/19), type it as two digits (02/19). If you make a mistake and enter an invalid date or time, the speaker will beep. You can backspace and correct the mistake.

The meaning of the various attributes are:

Read-Only (abbreviated "R" on the two-column display) – If a file is marked as Read-Only, then the file can't be changed or erased from DOS. Read-Only provides a good way of protecting files from being accidentally erased.

Hidden ("H") – If a file is marked as Hidden, it does not appear in a normal DOS DIRectory.

System ("S") – Like Hidden, a file marked as System does not appear in a normal DOS DIRectory. (The two DOS system files IBMBIO.COM and IBMDOS.COM are marked as both Hidden and System, and are not listed when you type DIR from DOS.)

Normal – If a file is not marked as Read-Only, Hidden, or System, PC Tools Deluxe labels it as Normal. (Not explicitly shown on the two-column display.)

Archive ("A") – The Archive attribute is used by the DOS BACKUP program (and the PC Tools Deluxe PCBACKUP program) to decide which files to back up. Whenever DOS makes any change to a file, it marks it as Archive, which means the changed file should be backed up. When BACKUP backs up a file, it unmarks it again, meaning it has now been backed up.

Once you've set attributes the way you want them, press "U" to make the changes. The new attributes will be recorded on the disk. You can also use the left and right arrow keys to select a different file. The left arrow key will display the previous file selected in the directory; the right arrow key will display the next file selected.

If you instead decide you don't want to change the attributes or time/date, press ESC.

MAPPING

The MAPPING option of PC Tools Deluxe lets you see which
sectors, or "clusters", of a disk are used by which files, and
which sectors are free for use. It is extremely useful in
determining if a file is non–contiguous, which can cause poor
system performance (more about this later in this section).

After you've selected the MAPPING option from the "Disk and
Special Functions" menu (press "F3" from the "File Functions"
menu) and an appropriate drive letter, the disk will whir and a
display similar to the following will appear:

```
PC Tools Deluxe - RX.xx                        Volume=None
---------------------File Mapping Service-------------------
Path=B:\*.*


Entire disk mapped
              Track    1   1   2   2   3   3   3
                   0   5   0   5   0   5   0   5   9
Double sided Bhhh.........................****
             Fhh..........................****
    Side 0   Fhh..........................****
             Dhh..........................****
    -----Dhh..............................****
             Dhh..........................****
    Side 1   hhh..........................*****
             hhh..........................*****
             hhh..........................*****

                  Explanation of Codes
             * Available          . Allocated
             B Boot record        h hidden
             F File Alloc Table    r Read Only
             D Directory          x Bad Cluster

             "F" to map files. ESC to return.
```

(Note: This is the floppy display. If you're mapping a hard disk,
the display will show only <u>allocated </u>clusters.)

Each position in the grid represents one cluster. PC DOS always allocates disk space for files a cluster at a time. One thing that complicates the disk storage is that clusters can be different sizes. On single–sided floppy disks, one cluster equals one sector. On double–sided disks, one cluster equals two sectors. On hard disks, clusters can be 4 or even 8 sectors long. Regardless of the size of a cluster for any given disk, PC DOS always sets aside disk space by clusters, not sectors.

For floppy disks, PC Tools Deluxe shows the corresponding track numbers above the grid (Track 0, 5, 10, 15, etc.). If you're mapping a single–sided disk, the actual sector numbers are also shown on the left. For hard disks, the clusters are shown in a large grid, without track numbers (since different hard disks use tracks and sectors in different ways).

Each space in the grid contains a symbol, showing what that cluster is used for. Here is an elaboration of the codes shown for the above example (the codes in the manual may be different from screen codes as IBM graphics characters are used to make the display more readable):

<u>*</u> Available – This cluster is available for file storage. It is not being used right now.

<u>B</u> Boot record – This cluster contains the boot record. Every disk contains a boot record, even if it is not capable of booting DOS.

<u>F</u> File Alloc Table – This cluster holds part of the File Allocation Table (FAT), which is used to keep track of where files are stored on the disk and which clusters are available.

<u>D</u> Directory – This cluster is part of the disk's directory.

<u>.</u> Allocated – This cluster is part of a file.

<u>h</u> hidden – This cluster is part of a hidden file.

70

r Read Only – This cluster is part of a Read–Only file.

x Bad Cluster – This cluster has been marked as bad and unusable.

(For more information on how files are stored on disk, please refer to your IBM Disk Operating System Manual.)

If you want to see which clusters are used by specific files, press "F". If the disk contains subdirectories, a subdirectory "tree" display will appear for you to select the subdirectory containing the files you want to map.

Then the files for that directory will appear. Notice the help line at the bottom of the screen:

```
Select file(s) to be mapped and then press "G" to proceed.
F8=directory LIST argument  F9=file SELECTion argument  F10-chg path
   ^v=scroll  <+=SELECT  F1=UNselect  F2=alt dir 1st  Esc=exit
```

Select the first file you want to map. If you don't select a file, PC Tools Deluxe will assume you want to start with the first entry of the directory.

Press "G". The disk map will reappear, but only the clusters used by the one file will be shown in the map. Notice the filename on the left, and the new help lines at the bottom:

```
      Use arrows(<-- -->) to view other files.
"D" to view entire disk map. "F" to reselect files. ESC to return.
```

If you press the right or left arrow keys, the next or previous file (respectively) will be shown on the map. Using these features, you can see what clusters on the disk any given file uses. If you want to view the entire disk map again, and return to the file map, press "D". If you want to select a different starting file (or a different directory if the disk contains subdirectories), press "F" again. When you're finished viewing the map, press ESC to exit.

If, when mapping a file, you see that the clusters are not contiguous, you may wish to use the PC Tools Deluxe COMPRESS option to unfragment your hard disk. It takes longer to access a file when its clusters are not contiguous due to increased head movement. Compress will optimize disk performance and make file undeleting as reliable as possible.

SYSTEM INFO

The SYSTEM INFO option of PC Tools Deluxe provides useful information about your computer. When you select the SYSTEM INFO option, there may be a short pause, then a display similar to the following will appear:

```
PC Tools Deluxe - RX.xx
-----------------System Information Service------------------

                           Computer - Laser Compact XTE
             The BIOS programs are dated - 01/01/86
                   Operating system - DOS 3.3
        Number of logical disk drives - 4
         Logical drive letter range - A thru D
                       Serial Ports - 2
                     Parallel Ports - 2
                           CPU Type - 8088
         Relative speed (orig PC=100%) - 210%
           Math Co-processor present - no
User programs are loaded at HEX paragraph - 0600
Memory used by DOS and resident programs - 84736 bytes
     Memory available for user programs - 570624 bytes
         Total memory reported by DOS - 640K
PC Tools has found the total memory to be - 640K
             Extended Memory Installed - 1024K
             Expanded Memory Installed - 512K, in use - 256K

                    Display Adapter present - Monochrome
Additional ROM BIOS found at hex paragraph - C800

Press any key to return
```

The meanings of some of these items are fairly obvious. Here are brief descriptions of each item:

Computer – PC Tools Deluxe can "recognize" all of the IBM models and many PC compatibles by looking at a signature byte on the ROM/BIOS. If PC Tools Deluxe does not know what computer this is, it does not display this line.

The BIOS programs are dated – This tells you when the built-in BIOS (Basic Input/Output System) firmware was last changed.

PC Tools Deluxe

This can be useful for comparing computers, since the manufacturer will change the BIOS date if the computer's BIOS is updated in any way.

Operating system – This lets you know which version of DOS you've booted.

Number of logical disk drives – This tells you how many drives are connected, including floppy drives, hard disks, RAM disks (electronic disks), etc. This number is also controlled with the "LASTDRIVE" option of your CONFIG.SYS FILE. The default may be "E" or 5 drives even if you really don't have five drives.

Logical drive letter range – Shows which drive letter names are allowable for the drives you have connected.

Serial Ports – Number of serial ports connected.

Parallel Ports – Number of parallel ports connected.

CPU Type – The type of processor installed (8088, 80286, etc.)

Relative Speed – The CPU processing speed as measured against the original IBM PC running at 4.77 MHZ. We perform a variety of machines instructions we feel is representative of normal application programming. Because speed tests vary, the reported relative speed may slightly differ from other applications which attempt to measure the CPU processing speed.

Math Co-processor present – PC Tools Deluxe will look for the math processor (regardless of system switch settings) and will indicate if it finds one.

User programs are loaded at HEX paragraph, and Memory used by DOS and resident programs – These two items are related, since the operating system uses the lowest area of memory and user programs load directly after this. The larger these numbers are, the more memory is being used by the operating system (along with any resident programs loaded before PC Tools Deluxe) and the less memory is available for user programs. Note that if you are using PC Tools Deluxe in its resident mode, this will display the size of the operating system and resident programs up to (but not including) PC Tools Deluxe. If you have other resident programs that were started after PC Tools Deluxe, they will not be included as operating system memory either.

Memory available for user programs – This is the amount of memory available for user programs (such as PC Tools Deluxe, word processors, spread sheets, etc). Note that if you have PC Tools Deluxe resident, it will not reflect the amount of memory taken up by PC Tools Deluxe, so real available memory will be less by the amount you specified with the "/RxxxK" command when you started PC Tools Deluxe (usually 64K).

Total memory reported by DOS – This is the amount of memory which DOS believes to be available, which may or may not be all of the computer's memory. See the next item.

PC Tools has found the total memory to be – PC Tools Deluxe ignores any memory switch settings and determines for itself how much memory is available in the computer (up to 640K). If the two numbers disagree, then you know that either the switches in your computer are set wrong, or else a program such as a RAM disk or print spooler has taken some of the memory for itself and "lied" to DOS about the amount of available memory.

Extended Memory installed – The amount of Extended memory found (if any) by PC Tools Deluxe.

Expanded Memory installed – The amount of Lotus/Intel/Microsoft expanded memory (EMS) found by PC Tools Deluxe.

PC Tools Deluxe

In use – The amount of EMS memory currently in use.

Display Type – PC Tools Deluxe will print the current display adapter type (instead of the words "Display Type"). It recognizes CGA, EGA, Mono, VGA, and PGA adapters. It will also display the amount of memory for EGA displays.

Additional ROM BIOS found at HEX Paragraph – This lets you know if any expansion boards are plugged into your PC that contain "extensions" to the PC BIOS. If none are found, this line will not be displayed. For example, the IBM PC/XT hard disk controller board contains ROM code for the hard disk that uses this BIOS extension protocol.

PRINT

The PRINT option of PC Tools Deluxe allows you to print out any file as a standard text file or "dumped" as hexadecimal values and ASCII characters. It also has an option to print with page formatting. To begin, select the correct drive, subdirectory, and file(s) as described earlier in this chapter.

Press "P" for "Print". For each file you've selected, you'll see:

```
PC Tools Deluxe - RX.xx                    Volume Label=None
---------------------File Print Service----------------------
Path=B:\

File=FILENAME.EXT

Please specify your print options as follows:

"P" - print as a standard text file (file contains control
  characters as necessary)
"W" - print as a standard text file (using PCTools print options)
"D" - each sector DUMPED in ASCII and HEX
"N" - skip this file and go to next one selected
ESC - return
```

To print the file, make sure your printer is on, then press "P" to print the file as text without page formatting; "W" to select margins, line spacing, and headers before printing; or "D" to print it as a dump of hex and ASCII values (similar to the VIEW/EDIT display). You can stop the printing at any time if you need to by pressing ESC.

If you don't want to print the selected file, press "N" to skip to the next selected file. To exit the PRINT option, press ESC.

If you select the "W" option for formatted printing (usually to print documents created with the PC Tools Deluxe Word Processor), you will see a screen with the following options:

PC Tools Deluxe

```
Lines per page              66  |  Page headings (Y or N)        N
Margin lines top & bottom    4  |  Page footings (Y or N)        N
Extra spaces between lines   0  |  Page numbers  (y or N)        N
Left margin                  1  |  Want to stop between Pages?   Y
Right margin               080  |  Want to eject last page?      Y
Line length is 080 characters   |  Printer options are correct
```

Use the arrow keys to move to any options you want to change, then press the RETURN key. A cursor will appear over the option. Enter the new value then press return again. When all options are set correctly, move the highlighted bar over the "print options are correct" line then press RETURN again. PC Tools Deluxe will ask you to make sure your printer and paper are ready, then will print your document for you.

Note: The PRINT option can only print files. If you want to print directory listings, use the List option from the "File Functions" menu. If you wish to print the contents of the screen, press shift–PrtSc.

LOCATE

If you have disks with subdirectories, LOCATE can help you find
which subdirectories contain which files. Suppose you're looking
for a certain file, but can't remember which subdirectory it is in.
LOCATE will search all subdirectories on the disk, looking for
the filename. This is especially helpful when you're working with
hard disks, which may contain many subdirectories and files.

When you select LOCATE from the "Disk and Special
Functions" menu and an appropriate drive letter, this display will
appear:

```
PC Tools Deluxe - RX.xx
-------------------File Locater Service----------------------
Path=B:\

     Enter the name and/or extension to be used as a search
     argument for the directory listing. A question mark (?)
     is a "WILDCARD" which will always match any character
     found in that position. An asterisk in the name or
     extension will match that position and all remaining
     positions.

          Name=[*      ]
          Ext =[*   ]

     Name and extension correct as entered, (Y/N)?  [y]

     Press ESC to Exit
```

If you're looking for a single file, just enter the filename and
extension. If you're looking for several files with similar names,
you can use the "wildcard" characters "*" and "?".

After you've entered the desired filename, answer the (Y/N)
question with "Y". PC Tools Deluxe will begin to search each
subdirectory on the disk, showing you the directory it's currently
searching. For every matching file it finds, it displays a "directory
entry" line for that file. You can read the entire pathname for the
file.

PC Tools Deluxe

The LOCATE option is also convenient for seeing a directory of the entire disk. If you enter "*.*" for the filename, PC Tools Deluxe will show you every file in every subdirectory on the disk.

INITIALIZE (FORMAT)

The INITIALIZE (Format) option of PC Tools Deluxe allows you
to format a new data diskette. Brand new disks must be
formatted before they can be used for saving files. Formatting
writes special information onto every track of the disk so that
your computer can recognize this as an IBM DOS disk.
Formatting also completely erases anything that was on the disk
before.

The Initialize option can be especially convenient if the PC Tools
Deluxe program is resident in memory. For example, suppose
you're working on a new word processor document, and
suddenly realize that you don't have an available disk on which to
save the file. Without PC Tools Deluxe, you might have to exit
the word processor (losing the document you were working on),
format a new disk from DOS, start the word processor again,
retype the text all over again, then save the file. With PC Tools
Deluxe resident in memory, however, just press CTRL-ESC to
start up PC Tools Deluxe, use the INITIALIZE option to format a
new disk, exit out of PC Tools Deluxe right back to your waiting
word processor program, then save the text!

(Note: The INITIALIZE option is designed for formatting new data
disks. It does not make bootable disks. You can, if you are using
IBM PC DOS (not MS–DOS), turn a disk formatted with PC
Tools Deluxe into a bootable disk using the DOS "SYS"
command and copying the "COMMAND.COM" file to the newly
formatted disk. Complete instructions are given by the PC Tools
Deluxe FORMAT option.)

Select "N" for "iNitialize" from the "Disk and Special Functions"
menu. Next, select the drive letter that contains the disk to be
formatted. The following display will appear:

PC Tools Deluxe

```
PC Tools Deluxe - RX.xx
-------------------Disk Initialization Service----------------

      Drive B is about to be initialized (formatted).

      Choose the formatting desired
      and press ENTER to begin.

      360K<--->Double-sided, 9 sectors per track
      320K
      180K
      160K



Press ESC to Exit
```

The possible formatting options are:

720K –	3 1/2 diskette, 80 tracks, Double–sided, 9 sectors per track,
360K –	Double–sided, 9 sectors per track, 40 tracks
320K –	Double–sided, 8 sectors per track, 40 tracks
180K –	Single–sided, 9 sectors per track, 40 tracks
160K –	Single–sided, 8 sectors per track, 40 tracks
1.2M –	AT high capacity, 80 tracks, Double–sided, 15 sectors per track
1.4M –	PS/2 Models 50, 60, and 80 format, Double–sided, 18 sectors per track

The display will only give you those options that are possible on the given drive. The 1.2M and 1.44M options are supported only on machines with 80286 or 80386 processors. In addition, the 1.44M option will require PC DOS vers. 3.2 (or higher), or MS DOS vers. 3.3.

If you're going to be using this formatted disk on a computer with single–sided drives, you should select one of the single–sided options. If you'll be using this disk with DOS Version 1.0 or 1.1, you should select an 8–sector option, since DOS 1.0 and 1.1 do not work correctly with disks that use 9 sectors per track. The 1.2M format can only be selected if your computer is an AT and contains a high capacity drive. If you are formatting a 3 1/2 inch disk, select the 720K or 1.44M option as desired for the drive type you have.

Use the cursor keys to select the formatting option you want. Make sure the disk to be formatted is in the correct drive, then press Enter. PC Tools Deluxe will format the disk using the option you selected.

When the formatting is complete, PC Tools Deluxe will ask you if you wish to give the newly formatted disk the capability of being made bootable. If you select "Y", it will write boot information to the disk. This does take disk space so unless you plan to boot from the disk, we recommend not taking this option. If you do, it will not make the disk bootable; it will only write the boot record and reserve space for DOS on the disk. You will need to use the DOS "SYS" command and copy the file "COMMAND.COM" to the new disk before it can be booted. This, of course, can be done anytime later.

Note: This should work reliably with IBM PC–DOS. If using MS–DOS, it may be necessary to delete the IBMBIOS.COM and IBMDOS.COM "spaces" that PC Tools Deluxe creates on the target disk before running the DOS "SYS" command.

When the format operation is complete, the above display will reappear. You can either select to format another disk, or press ESC to exit to the "Disk and Special Functions" menu.

PC Tools Deluxe has one other advantage over the DOS FORMAT command: If it encounters any bad sectors, it will mark only those that are bad as unusable. The DOS FORMAT command will make the entire track that contains the bad sector unavailable.

Note: Generally, we recommend that you use the PCFORMAT command supplied with PC Tools Deluxe instead of the PC Tools internal disk formatter. PCFORMAT initializes disks (both

PC Tools Deluxe

floppy and hard disks) in such a way that the data, in most cases, can be recovered with the REBUILD command. Use the PC Tools Deluxe resident formatter only when you are in a jam and need a quick formatted disk.

PARK (Hard Disk)

Pressing the letter "P" from the Disk and Special Functions menu will park the hard disk head. This is recommended if you plan to move your computer as it will position the head over an unused portion of your hard disk. In the event a shock causes the head to "bounce" on the media, it will not damage any valuable data.

The hard disk head will be parked at the highest cylinder on the logical drive. On a partitioned hard disk this is at the end of the last partition.

Chapter 4 – COMPRESS

Introduction

The file COMPRESS.EXE is a program which will analyze a hard disk or floppy diskette for fragmentation and optionally correct it.

Compress doesn't compress the data in a file by shrinking strings of like characters, but instead compresses the files on a hard disk or diskette such that each file is contained in one contiguous area (unfragmented).

Fragmentation is the condition where the different parts of a file are not stored together on the disk. This can occur due to the way DOS allocates space for a new file or an old growing file. If there has been much file creation and deletion activity, then it's likely that some of the files are fragmented. There are two reasons that this is undesirable. First, if portions of a file are stored in widely separated areas of the disk, then accesses to that file will be slowed. Therefore, disk–intensive programs will perform better if the disk is compressed. Second, the Undelete facility of PC Tools Deluxe will sometimes be unable to recover files perfectly if the deleted files were fragmented and the delete tracking option of MIRROR was not installed.

SYSTEM REQUIREMENTS:
DOS: v2.0 or higher
Memory: up to 256K depending on size of disk
Files: 4,000 files or less

You may start the program by typing:

```
COMPRESS [C:] [/NM] [/BW] [/CU] [/CF] [/CC]
```

Where C: is the name of the disk to be compressed and is optional. If not specified, Compress will assume the current drive.

/NM will suppress the running of MIRROR after compress has completed.

/BW is also optional and will suppress colors on the screen while COMPRESS is running. If you have difficulty reading the color display on your monitor, /BW can improve its appearance. /BW is ignored for monochrome systems.

The /CU, /CF, and /CC options allow you to run the various compress option 5 features from a batch file without additional input. For example, typing:

```
COMPRESS  C:  /CU
```

will unfragment your hard disk using the "Unfragment and minimum compression" option. The /CF parameter will do a full compress and /CC will do a full compress and clear all unused sectors. See option 5 for more instructions.

The program is easy to use. The most helpful options are "0" (Set Sort Options), "5" (Compress), and "3" (Surface scan). Just follow the on-screen prompts. Here is a description of each of the options in COMPRESS:

Option 0 "Set Sort Options"

Select this function if you want to have Compress sort all your directories as it optimizes the disk. This option doesn't do the actual sorting. Rather, it defines the type of sort that will be performed by option 5 "Compress disk(ette)". The options available are:

Sort by **FILENAME**
Sort by file **EXTENSION**
Sort by File **SIZE**
Sort by **DATE/TIME**

In addition, you can select either an **ASCENDING** or **DESCENDING** sort sequence.

Selecting a sort option other than FILENAME will still sort by filename within each identical file group. For example, selecting to sort by ASCENDING EXTENSION will also sub–sort by filename when the extension is the same. For example, all your .COM files will appear before all .EXE files and DISKCOPY.COM will be listed before FORMAT.COM.

Note: The Sort option does not affect where the files are physically placed on the hard disk – it only sorts the file names within each directory. Compress will not physically move files except when it needs to remove file fragmentation and/or move all unused space to the back of the disk.

Option 1 "Disk(ette) analysis"

This option displays allocation information for the selected disk drive. It will show:

the number of allocated clusters (disk space in use)
the number of unallocated clusters (free disk space)
the number of bad clusters
the number of file chains (files and subdirectories)
the number of fragmented file chains
a percentage file fragmentation factor
the number of non–contiguous free space areas
the number of cross linked file chains
the number of unattached file clusters
the number of bad clusters within file chains

While much of this is technical information you don't need to worry about, some is useful to understand:

The number of FRAGMENTED FILE CHAINS lets you know how many of your files and subdirectories are fragmented. The next line of the display shows this as a percentage of the total number of file chains on the disk. The longer it has been since you have run Compress (option 5) the higher this number is likely to be. If it is zero, you don't have any fragmented files.

The number of NON–CONTIGUOUS FREE SPACE AREAS lets you know how many pieces your available space is divided into. It is desirable that this be kept small since the next time you create a file (or an existing file grows), DOS will allocate these pieces to the file. If there are many small pieces, instead of one large one, the new or enlarged file will likely be highly fragmented. This will make access to its data slow.

The last three items above indicate problems with your directories/file allocation table that only CHKDSK can correct.

Option 2 "Files analysis"

This option gives you more information on the possible fragmentation of individual files. If Option 1 shows that there are fragmented files, this option will tell you which ones they are. Each file is displayed along with the total number of clusters it occupies. It also shows the number of pieces the file is broken into (an unfragmented file has a "1") and the percentage of fragmentation for that file. Ordinarily, you won't need to run this option. If option 1 shows there are fragmented files, you can proceed directly to option 5 to compress the disk.

Option 3 "Surface scan"

The surface scan option is very useful to catch and mark marginal clusters as bad so that DOS will not attempt to store your data in areas that may turn up bad later. Normally, DOS will attempt several retries before it even alerts you (via the familiar "Abort, Retry, Ignore" type message) that a sector is bad. Surface scan will read each sector several times. If an error is found, it will mark this cluster as bad. If this cluster is already allocated to a file, it will attempt to move the data to a safe place first.

It is a good idea to run the surface scan option periodically as it can find bad spots _before_ DOS does and before you lose any data. Due to the complexity of the analysis it does, it can take several hours to run. This is a great option to start overnight and let run until you come back to your computer in the morning.

You can select either a set number of passes, or have the surface scan option run until the "ESC" key is pressed. When it is done, it will display a report which you can optionally send to your printer or to a file which must be on a drive other than the one being scanned.

Option 4 "Organization analysis"

This option will tell you whether or not a compression needs to be run, but will not actually start the compress option.

Option 5 "Compress disk(ette)"

This is the option that actually performs the disk optimization features and sorts your directories if you selected sort options. It does this by 1) removing any file fragmentation that may exist, and 2) moving free space to the back of the disk. Compress has three options:

COMPRESS Options

There are three types of disk compression. All three options will correct any file fragmentation.

The "Full compression" option will move every last cluster of free space to the back of the disk. Because of this, it might take slightly longer to run. For example, if your hard disk had one cluster of free space close to the front and you did not have any one cluster files near the back of the hard disk it could move forward to fill this hole, it would shift all the files on the hard disk one cluster forward to fill this gap. Moving all these files can take a long time, so we have provided a second option which provides most of the benefits of full compress but runs faster:

The "Unfragment and minimum compression" option works just like the Full compression option except that if it cannot find a small enough file to move forward, it will skip the gap and go on. In practice, this is likely to leave a few very small gaps of free space throughout your hard disk, with the vast majority of free space at the back. All files are unfragmented.

However, depending upon the makeup of files on your hard disk, you may find that there is little difference between the speed of the two options. For example, if you use your computer to write many letters, you probably have plenty of small files around to fill any gaps so compress won't have to resort to file shuffling. We recommend that you always run the Full compression option unless you find that it runs too slow on your disk. On most systems, if compress is run fairly often (at least once a week), we have found that it won't take more than a few minutes.

The last option, "Full Compression and Clear Free Clusters" does one more step: any free clusters are filled with zeros. Select this option if you want to make sure all deleted file data is physically removed from the hard disk. This should be done periodically as it makes REBUILD (if you are not using MIRROR) more reliable.

Important Notes

Running Mirror after Compress

After you have finished doing a disk compress, the Compress program will ask you if you wish to run Mirror (see the section on the MIRROR/REBUILD Utilities). If you have just compressed a fixed disk, you should always select "yes". Since Compress has moved your files and directories around, the Mirror file will no longer be current and will not reflect the actual status of your hard disk's data. Compress will look for the Mirror program in the current subdirectory and in the subdirectory the Compress program was run from.

Resident Software

Some types of resident programs, such as DOS's FASTOPEN, can be confused by the running of COMPRESS. Since COMPRESS moves files on the hard disk, it is highly recommended that you:

REBOOT after Compress is finished!

Unless this is done, it is possible that the next program you run will destroy your hard disk format and you will lose some or all of your data! Compress will print this warning each time it is finished to remind you.

Power Outage

Unlike most other hard disk optimizing programs, COMPRESS will not lose information if power is lost during operation. If you want to stop the disk compression while it is running, we still recommend you press the "ESC" key rather than doing a warm boot (CTRL–ALT–DEL) or turning off the power to the computer. In the event that your computer's power becomes disconnected, don't panic: All your data is intact, but it may be necessary to use the DOS "CHKDSK" command to remove traces of the prior Compress run. To do this, type "CHKDSK /F". If you see the prompt "Convert lost chains into files?", answer "n". Your hard disk data is now intact, although still fragmented since Compress did not finish. Restart Compress and let it run to completion.

Copy Protection / File Ordering

The order of directory entries is unchanged by compression, unless sorting has been specified with option 0 before running COMPRESS. But the physical order of disk files will be optimized as follows:

    a. System files
    b. Subdirectories
    c. All other files

"Hidden" files are not moved to make sure any copy–protected programs you have on your disk continue to run. Many copy–protections (especially on hard disk) employ the use of hidden files and sub–directories as part of the copy protection. If Compress were to move hidden files, some copy protected programs would not run.

Because of this, a file might still be technically "fragmented" after Compress is run. For example, if DOS started building a file right in front of a hidden file, then extended it right behind the hidden file, Compress would not move either the hidden file or the file fragmented across it. This is done to prevent Compress from taking an extremely long time to process (this happens very rarely). Also, PC Tools's undelete option will be able to span the hidden file so data will be recoverable after an accidental delete.

Deleted Files

Compression will destroy the last traces of any deleted files. If you want to use PC Tools Deluxe to Undelete any files, be sure to do so BEFORE compression. COMPRESS will clear the delete tracking file created by MIRROR, if it is found.

COMPRESS

Chapter 5 – Hard Disk BACKUP & RESTORE

Features

This section describes the utility programs PCBACKUP.EXE and PCRESTOR.EXE which are found on your PC Tools Deluxe diskette. The purpose of these programs is to make floppy diskette archival copies (backups) of your hard disk files and, when needed, to restore your hard disk files from the backups. These programs are similar to the DOS utilities BACKUP and RESTORE but are more convenient and much faster.

PCBACKUP features:

* Very fast operation.

* Automatic error recovery of up to 160 errors per disk.

* Format the floppy diskettes automatically during the backup.

* Backup all files, selected files or only altered files.

* Restore all files or only selected files.

* Verify that the backups are identical to the hard disk files.

* Will work with almost any kind of floppy drive, including 3.5 inch 720k drives, 5.25 inch 360k drives, 3.5 inch 1.44 Meg drives and 5.25 inch 1.2 Meg AT-type drives. PCBACKUP will use either one or two floppy drives providing they are the same type. PCRESTOR will use only one floppy drive.

* PCBACKUP will backup up to the following rates (depending upon file sizes, buffer size, etc.):
  – PC type computer with 360K drive – 1250K per minute.
  – AT type computer with 1.2 meg drive – 2250K per minute.

PCBACKUP

Note: Backups created in a 1.2 meg drive on 360K media will not restore reliably from a 360K drive. This is a limitation of the 1.2 meg drive.

System Requirements:

A hard disk, of course. One or more floppy drives.

At least 128 K bytes of free memory. DOS version 2.00 or higher.

For faster operation, we recommend ten or more DOS buffers. This is selected in your system's configuration file CONFIG.SYS (e.g. BUFFERS=10). If your hard disk contains groups of many small files, you may want to increase this number further. (e.g. BUFFERS=20)

Introduction

PCBACKUP and PCRESTOR operate much faster than the DOS Backup and Restore commands. Much of the speed increase is a result of running the hard disk and the floppy drives simultaneously. In other words, while the computer is waiting for the floppy disk controller chip inside your computer to write the data to the backup disk, it is retrieving more data from the hard disk. Therefore, as PCBACKUP runs, you will notice that both the hard disk and floppy drive lights are on at the same time.

Another way PCBACKUP gains performance over the DOS Backup command is to leave the floppy drive on during the entire time the backup is being made. This minimizes time it has to wait for the drive to "come up to speed". It also allows PCBACKUP to detect disk inserts. You will notice that you never have to press any keys during the backup procedure. PCBACKUP can automatically tell when you remove or insert diskettes.

PCBACKUP is very flexible. It will create a "log" file as it makes a backup that quickly tells it what files were last backed up. This log file is used by PCRESTOR to quickly locate files and data on the backup diskettes without first having to scan the disks. However, the log file is not required. If PCRESTOR can't find the log, it will build one itself as it runs. This is slightly slower, but means that you can recover your data no matter what happens to the log file stored on your hard disk.

In addition to making simple backups, PCBACKUP can be used to quickly transfer data from one system to another. All you need is the PCRESTOR program, the log file (PCBACKUP.LOG) and your backup diskettes. During the restore process to a new drive, PCRESTOR will automatically create any subdirectories for you and put your files into them, just as they were on the original hard disk drive. This is also helpful if your hard disk ever "crashes" and you need to restore all your data after a format.

PCBACKUP is also compatible with the widest range of computers possible. Since not all IBM PC compatible computers support running the floppy and hard disk simultaneously, it can run in a more standard fashion. While slower, this makes sure you can transfer your data to another computer if you need to. Further, PCBACKUP will usually detect whether it needs to change modes automatically so you don't need to worry about the details of your computer's DMA (direct memory access) circuitry.

PCBACKUP

Using PCBACKUP

Before beginning, the floppy disks that will hold the hard disk data, should be pre–numbered and inserted in order when prompted. PCBACKUP will format the disks as it goes. The format used by PCBACKUP is non–standard in order to improve performance and provide for error recovery and will be unreadable by DOS.

Start the program by typing:

> PCBACKUP C: (where C: is your hard disk).

If your hard disk is partitioned, backup each partition seperately.

You may quit the program at any time by pressing the Esc key.

The Configuration File

The first time that you run PCBACKUP (or whenever it cannot find its configuration file), it will ask you some questions about your diskette drives. PCBACKUP can use either one or two floppy drives to make the backups. If you have two floppy drives which support identical media and capacities, then you may use them both. PCBACKUP will write to one drive while you are swapping diskettes in the other. This speeds up the backup process.

When you have answered the questions about your disk drives, PCBACKUP will display the configuration and give you the chance to either accept or change it. If you accept it, the program will assume the choices are correct and ask you if you wish to save this configuration. If you answer Y, it will write the configuration information into a file named PCBACKUP.CFG in the root directory; if you answer N, it will use the configuration this one time but then forget it afterwards.

Once a configuration is saved, PCBACKUP won't need to ask about it again (neither will PCRESTOR, since it uses that same configuration file).

The Log file

When PCBACKUP is run it creates a "log" file: a record of the files it is backing up. PCRESTOR uses this information to restore the data from the floppy disks to the hard disk. The log file can be stored in the current subdirectory or the Root directory (selected from the configuration menu). If your hard disk is partitioned, you may wish to store each log file in it's own partition, rather than the root or current subdirectory of the first partition. To do this, simply call PCBACKUP from **that** partition (e.g. C>PCBACKUP C: or D>PCBACKUP D:). The log file can also be optionally saved to a formatted floppy disk at the end of the backup process. If PCBACKUP.LOG is not found in the root directory or current subdirectory, a new one will be created from the backup disks during the restore process.

Selecting Files to Backup

You will next be presented with the Backup Specifications display. This is where you may select the files to be backed up. You may press "Y" to modify any or all of the displayed choices; follow the instructions on the screen. If you accept the standard specifications, then ALL files on the hard disk will be backed up and a new log file is created. (The old log file will be renamed PCBACKUP.OLD.)

Here is a description of the options PCBACKUP will allow you to change:

Drive letter:	the drive to backup
Path:	the full path name of the directory to backup

101

Backup which files?   enter the file name or use the standard
                              DOSwildcard characters to select the files
                              to backup

You will also be able to select whether to backup any
subdirectories of the path you have chosen or not. For example,
if you specified the root directory, you can backup all
subdirectories in your root directory by selecting "Y". You can
also backup ALL files or only the files that have been changed
since the last time you made a backup. PCBACKUP will update
the directory "archive" indicators so it will know which files have
and have not been saved.

When you have selected the files you wish to backup, press "B"
to begin.

After a moment, you will see the words "Backing up <path>"
with at least one filename beneath it. The paths being backed up
will be displayed in color (or highlighted), with the files
underneath and indented. At the bottom of the screen will
appear one of the following messages:

```
Remove diskette from drive <d>
Insert new backup diskette <n> in drive <d>
Insert backup diskette <n> in drive <d>
Writing backup diskette <n> in drive <n>
Formatting + writing backup diskette <n> in drive <d>
```

Which message you see will depend upon 1) Was there a
diskette already in the drive? If so, was it a diskette created by
PCBACKUP or some other diskette?, and 2) the type of backup
you are making.

PCBACKUP will first check to see if there is a diskette already in
the drive <d> that you have specified. If there is, it will check to
see whether it was made by PCBACKUP or some other program.
PCBACKUP uses a special disk format so it can reliably
distinguish between its own disks and DOS disks. This prevents
accidentally erasing an important disk that happened to be in the
drive when you started PCBACKUP. If it detects a non-backup

diskette, it will instruct you to remove the disk, then give you the prompt to insert the backup disk in the drive. If the disk was one you want to overwrite, you can insert it again. PCBACKUP will assume that if you put it back in the drive that you know what you are doing.

If the diskettes you are using are either new or were formatted by another program such as DOS, then you will see the message "Formatting + writing backup diskette <n> in drive <d>". This means that PCBACKUP is formatting or reformatting the diskette with its special format before writing your data to the disk. This slows the backup down considerably, but only happens the first time you use your backup diskettes. For this reason, we suggest that you keep one or more sets of diskettes that you will use with PCBACKUP. Subsequent backups will run much faster since the diskettes will already be formatted.

Once you insert the first backup diskettes, you will notice the "Kilobytes written" number at the bottom of the screen start to change. This records the total amount of data PCBACKUP has written to your diskettes during this backup session. Note that since PCBACKUP is also writing some "control" information that it uses internally, this number will be about 10 percent larger than the size of all your files.

Two timers at the bottom of the screen will also be running. These keep track of the total elapsed time (total backup time plus the time it waited for you to insert diskettes) and the total waiting time.

When PCBACKUP has finished writing the first diskette, it will ask you to remove it from the drive. When you have done so, it will ask you to insert the next disk, and will continue making your backup. When all the files you have requested are backed up, it will display the message:

"backup complete. Press any key to end".

When you press a key, PCBACKUP will tell you the rate that data was transferred to your backup disks in kilobytes and the number of diskettes used.

It will also display a very important warning:

"CAUTION.....
If this is your first backup run or if you have just used diskettes that have never before been written to with PCBACKUP, it is HIGHLY recommended that you run PCRESTOR with the <u>verify</u> option to ensure the quality of the diskettes. You may not discover a bad diskette until you really need it."

Please note: The "verify" portion of PCRESTOR is a seperate operation which should be performed before actually restoring the diskettes to the hard disk.

Here's why this is so important:

PCBACKUP (like all other fast hard disk backup programs) does not actually verify the data it has written to the diskette. This extra verification would make the backup process so slow you probably would never use it. Instead, PCBACKUP writes an extra "parity" sector on each track of every diskette it uses. This parity sector can be used to recover all data even if there was one error on every track of the backup disk.

The problem occurs when there is more than one error per track. In this case, PCRESTOR won't be able to recover, and the file that was written there will be bad. (This same limitation applies to Fastback™ or any other high-speed disk backup program.)

Normally, disk errors (if the media is of high quality) are very rare. In most cases, you won't get any errors even if your backup spans 50 or more diskettes. However, if the diskettes you are using are not good, you might not find out until your hard disk crashes and you really need them.

Also we recommend that you periodically clean your floppy drive heads using a disk head cleaning kit, available from most computer stores.

If, the first time the backup disks are used, you verify them with PCRESTOR, you can continue to use them for future backups with a very high degree of confidence that you will be able to recover your data.

Total, Partial, and Incremental Backups

PCBACKUP can make three different kinds of backups: Total, Partial, and Incremental. The type is determined by your selection of the files to be backed up:

Total = backup all files from all directories. PCBACKUP assumes you want to make a total backup when you specify a path of the root directory and all files (*.*). When a total backup is done, a new PCBACKUP.LOG file is created and the backup begins with diskette number 001. The previous contents of the backup diskettes are overwritten and lost. The original file log is renamed PCBACKUP.OLD.

Partial = backup only selected files. PCBACKUP assumes you want to make a partial backup if you select specific files or paths. A partial backup is just like an incremental backup except that specific files are "forced" to be saved regardless of the setting of the Archive status.

Incremental = backup only modified files and add them to existing diskettes. PCBACKUP assumes you want to make an incremental backup when you change the archive status to "M" to select modified files only. This type of backup is made when there is an existing log file (previous backups have been made). The previous contents of the backup diskettes are preserved, which allows PCRESTOR to recover files from past backup

105

sessions. The new backup will be appended to the end of the existing backup diskettes. Since data is being added, you will most likely need additional backup diskettes.

Incremental and partial backups are usually done to save the time it takes to make daily backups. For example, you could make a total backup every day, or you could make a total backup on Monday, and an incremental backup on Tuesday through Friday, backing up only the files that have changed. The procedure you would follow would be the same, except on Tuesday through Friday, you would instruct PCBACKUP to backup only modified files by changing the "A" to an "M" at the PCBACKUP menu.

Command Line Options

It is possible to select each item of the Backup Specifications display from the DOS command line. This is NOT required and usually only the drive letter should be entered on the command line. But if you wish to run PCBACKUP from a DOS batch file, the command format is:

```
PCBACKUP C: PATH=\pathname FILES=filename.ext /DL /NS /M /NU /C /NO
                                                                  /B
```

or

```
PCBACKUP C: @\pathname\filename.ext  /DL  /NO  /C
```

The meaning of each option is described below. All except /C, /B, /NO and /DL are presented on the Backup Specifications display and can be changed there.

C: Drive letter of the hard disk.

pathname. The DOS path to the particular subdirectory you wish to back up. If specified, it must start with a reverse slash (\) and begin at the root directory. This is used to restrict the backup to the files contained in the path. If a path is not specified, then the backup will begin with the files in the root directory and, unless /NS is used, will also include all the files in all subdirectories.

filename. Name of the file(s) you wish to back up. Normally all files are backed up, regardless of their names. This option restricts the backup to only those files having this name or, if you use the wildcard characters * or ?, to a group of files with similar names.

.ext   Extension to the filename. This option restricts the backup to only those files with this extension or, if you use the wildcard characters * or ?, to those files with similar extensions. Normally files are backed up regardless of their extensions.

/NS No Subdirectories. This restricts the backup to only those files in the one selected directory. Normally, files from all of the selected path's subdirectories are also backed up.

/M Modified files only. This restricts the backup to those files which have been written or altered since the last backup (we call this an 'incremental' backup). Normally this distinction is ignored, and all files are backed up even if their "archive flags" indicate that they are unchanged since the last backup.

/NU No Update of the "archive flags". Normally each hard disk archive flag is updated (cleared to 0) after that file has been backed up.

/C. The hardware configuration menu is displayed, even if the configuration file PCBACKUP.CFG already exists. This allows you to override or change the previous configuration. Normally that menu is displayed only if the file PCBACKUP.CFG cannot be found in the root directory of the current drive. This option is available only on the DOS command line.

PCBACKUP

/NO. No overlap. This manually turns off the use of simultaneous hard disk and floppy disk DMA (direct memory access). With this option, backups will be slower, but will work on machines that are not capable of simultaneous DMA due to limitations in their circuitry. PCBACKUP will automatically detect most computers that need this option and will display a menu asking you whether you want to run in "no overlap" mode, try slowing the processor speed (if the computer has multiple speeds, this can sometimes help), or try the backup in overlap mode anyway. You should try the "/NO" option only if your computer is "hanging" or otherwise acting oddly during the backup or restore process.

/DL. Delete Log. This will override PCBACKUP's assumptions about when to do an incremental backup. If the /DL parameter is specified, any existing LOG file will be renamed to PCBACKUP.OLD before the backup is run, thereby forcing a partial or full backup. The backup disks will be completely overwritten and any existing data will be lost. Deleting the log file is useful when making a second backup of the same data, having a separate set of disks for a particular subdirectory, or if the data from the first backup is no longer needed.

/B. Batch file mode. The backup process will begin immediately without waiting for you to press any keys. All desired options (for example: PATH) must be included on the DOS command line unless the normal, standard selections are adequate. If the backup process is completed without errors, then control is returned directly to DOS. This option is available only on the DOS command line.

Response Files (@ Files)

The second form of the command line shown allows you to specify a "response file" that contains the rest of the command line options. This is very useful when you have specific files in various subdirectories that you want to backup and the "files" and "path" command line options do not provide enough flexibility.

For example, assume you want to backup all your Lotus 123 data files in the subdirectory "Lotus" and all your Microsoft Word data files in the subdirectory "Word". You couldn't do this on a single command line (as there are two different paths and different file specifications). You could run PCBACKUP twice. Or you could create a response file to do the work for you. To continue with the same example, the following command line:

PCBACKUP @\PCTOOLS\BACKUP.OPT /DL

tells PCBACKUP to do a partial backup and to look for the specific backup information in the response file called "BACKUP.OPT" in the directory "PCTOOLS". Additionally, since the /DL option is specified, it will create a new log file and start the backup with diskette #1. To backup Lotus and Word data files, the BACKUP.OPT file might look like this:

PATH=\LOTUS FILES=*.WK1 /NS
PATH=\WORD FILES=*.DOC /NS /M

Notice that each line of the response file contains exactly the same parameters that you would specify on the command line when running PCBACKUP directly. The difference is that a response file can have more than one line, each line being equivalent to a separate run of PCBACKUP. The bytes written to the backup diskettes will include header, path and file information from each line in the response file, in addition to data. This may slightly increase the amount of disk space used over the "Menu Method".

  The above example says to look in the subdirectory called "Lotus" for all files with an extension of "WK1" (the extension used by 123 data files). The /NS says "don't look in any subdirectories of the directory called Lotus". The next line instructs PCBACKUP to look in the subdirectory called "Word" for all files with an extension of "DOC" (the extension used by Microsoft Word documents). The /M says "only backup files that have been modified since the last backup."

You can create a response file using your favorite text editor (such as the Word Processor in PC Tools Deluxe) or use the DOS COPY command. To create the above response file using DOS, you could type:

```
COPY CON: BACKUP.OPT
PATH=\LOTUS FILES=*WK1 /NS
PATH=\WORD FILES=*.DOC /NS /M
F6    (press the F6 function key to end)
```

Note: The drive letter and the "/DL" parameter (if used) cannot be specified in the response file – they must be on the command line itself.

Other Information about Backups

1. If PCBACKUP "hangs" or the backup disks don't verify successfully with PCRESTOR try one or more of the following:
   - set the computer at slow speed (if dual speed processor)
   - boot the computer with an unmodified DOS disk from drive A to clear resident programs
   - use the /NO parameter (no overlap) which will force PCBACKUP to read from the hard disk and write to the floppy disks separately
   - use high quality floppy diskettes

2. Don't make a new Total backup using the same diskettes which hold your previous Total backup. Since a Total backup destroys the previous contents of the disks, the danger exists that if something goes wrong, you would lose both the new and old backup. Instead, for a total backup you should use a different group of disks: after successful completion of the new backup you may then re-use the older group of disks.

3. Backups may be made as often as desired or, conversely, as seldom as you dare. We suggest periodic (about once a week) 'total' backups combined with more frequent incremental (only modified files) backups.

4. Label each diskette with something like "Backup disk # <number>". The numbering of the diskettes is important, since PCBACKUP and PCRESTOR will always ask for each diskette by its number. If you mix up unlabeled diskettes, you'll have to try each one until the program recognizes the one it needs.

5. **Caution:** Do NOT attempt to use PCBACKUP (or PCRESTOR) with drives affected by the DOS utilities JOIN, SUBST, or ASSIGN.

   PCBACKUP cannot backup a subdirectory that has been given a logical drive letter (i.e. Lotus sub–dir recognized as drive D) with SUBST because PCRESTOR will not recognize it as a subdirectory and would restore to the Root directory. But the entire hard disk can be backed up even though this command has been used.

6. **Partitioned Drives:** If your hard drive is partitioned don't attempt to backup all partitions at once using the assign command. You must backup each partition separately. If you use Assign, PCRESTOR won't know where to put your data and will attempt to restore it to your first partition. Also, you may wish to store each log file in it's own partition, rather than the root directory of the first partition, for example. To do this, simply call PCBACKUP from that partition. (e.g. C>PCBACKUP C: or D>PCBACKUP D:)

7. PCBACKUP will always put and look for its LOG and CFG files in the ROOT directory. This is a change from previous versions of PCBACKUP that required them to be in the current directory.

Using PCRESTOR

The PCRESTOR program is used primarily to restore hard disk files from the floppy diskette backups made previously by the PCBACKUP program. PCRESTOR can also verify that backup files on the diskettes are identical to files on the hard disk.

Start the program by typing

   PCRESTOR C:

(where C: is your hard disk).

You can also specify the /C and /NO options described in the PCBACKUP section.

You may quit the program at any time by pressing the Esc key.

If the PCRESTOR program does not find the configuration file (PCBACKUP.CFG) in the root directory of the current drive, it will ask you some questions about your floppy drives (just as PCBACKUP would). Regardless of the number of drives specified in the PCBACKUP.CFG file, PCRESTOR will use only the first drive.

If PCRESTOR finds the log file (PCBACKUP.LOG) in the root directory of the current drive, it will read the information contained in it. But if the log file is not found, PCRESTOR must create it by reading the backup floppy diskettes and it will ask you to insert one or more of them, by number. If you wish to use a log file from a floppy disk, it must first be copied to the hard disk.

You will next see the PCRESTOR main menu.

On the left side of your screen is a list of the files you have backed up in the past. This list was read from the log file (or the backup diskettes, if the log file was missing). The file sizes, dates and times are displayed.

On the right side of your screen is a corresponding list of the files currently on your hard disk. If a file is found on your hard disk with the same name and path as a log file entry, then that hard disk file is listed on the right side. But if no such corresponding file is found, then there will be a blank line on the right side.

Above the left side of your screen will appear three pieces of information: the path name, the 'selection argument' and the 'set' number. The displayed path name is the path on the hard disk where the file was located at the time it was backed up. This same path on the hard disk is searched for the files to list on the right side. The 'file selection argument' (usually *.*) is described with the F8 function key below. The 'set' number is a convention used by PCRESTOR to display the backed up files in convenient groups: a new 'set' begins with each backup session and also with each different path within a backup session.

The central column contains codes describing the relationship between a backup file on the left and a hard disk file on the right. At various stages of operation this column may be used in any of these ways:

Backup file	=	Hard disk file	These files have equal dates & times.
Backup file	>	Hard disk file	The backup file is the newer one.
Backup file	<	Hard disk file	The backup file is the older.
Backup file	V	Hard disk file	Verified files have identical data.
Backup file	E	Hard disk file	The files did not verify as identical.
Backup file	R	Hard disk file	The hard disk file has been restored.
Backup file	S	Hard disk file	Same date & time, but sizes are different
Backup file		(blank)	Hard disk file was not found.

PC Tools Deluxe

The lower part of the screen lists the various keys you may press and the functions which they perform.

The Esc key stops the current operation; if none is in progress, it quits the program.

You may scroll through the file list with the up/down arrow keys. For quicker movement, the PgUp and PgDn keys jump by several files at a time. The Home and End keys jump to the top and bottom of the current 'set'.

VERIFY mode means that the backed up files on the floppy diskettes will be compared, for identical size and data content, with their counterparts on the hard disk which have the same paths and names. No files are altered.

RESTORE mode means that the backup files will be read from the diskettes and then written to your hard disk. If a file of that name already exists on your hard disk, then you will be prompted with various options before the hard disk file is replaced. No action is taken until you press F1, F2 or F3.

F7 allows you to select a different hard drive.

F8 allows you to specify the 'file selection argument'. This restricts, by their names, the files to be displayed and also to be verified or restored. The normal rule is *.* (no restrictions by file name; display all files).

F9 and **F10** are used to move forward and backward through the 'sets' of files.

HOME and **END** will move you to the beginning and end of the current 'set' (subdirectory) of files.

CTRL–HOME and **CTRL–END** will move you to the first and last 'sets' (subdirectories) of files.

F1, F2 and **F3** begin the disk operations, either Verify or Restore, depending upon the currently displayed Mode:

F1 for all files on the backup diskettes (may be restricted by F8).
F2 for only files in the current set (may be further restricted by F8).
F3 for only the one file selected by the moving display 'bar'.

Note: The F1 and F2 keys will backup files starting with the file noted by the inverse bar. If you want to skip some files, you can move the bar down before pressing the F1 or F2 keys to start.

If the files to be restored already exist on the drive, PCRESTOR will alert you and present a menu giving you several options to select whether to replace or retain the existing files.

Important Notes:

1. Nothing happens until you select either "VERIFY" or "RESTORE", then start the backup process with one of the function keys F1–F3.

2. If one of your backup disks is lost or damaged, you can still restore the files not contained on this disk: When PCRESTOR asks for the missing disk #, just insert the next disk. It will ask you if you are sure, then continue.

PCBACKUP

PC Tools Deluxe

Chapter 6 – MIRROR, REBUILD & PCFORMAT

*** WARNING! ***

REBUILD is intended to be used ONLY when needed to recover from a disastrous mistake! REBUILD rebuilds your hard disk's FAT and root from the file created by MIRROR or if MIRROR was not run, from the hard disk data itself. <u>Run this program only immediately after an accidental ERASE *.* RECOVER *.* or FORMAT.</u>

<u>Casual use of REBUILD is dangerous.</u> It is very important to understand that REBUILD depends upon the backup file written by MIRROR: it simply restores the entire FAT and the entire root directory to the state recorded in the backup file. If you have not recently used MIRROR then you will definitely lose new files created since the last time you used MIRROR and you may also lose some other data as well. If you have not been running MIRROR, then REBUILD can be even more dangerous, as it will create a new root directory and FAT based upon data it finds on the disk. Use REBUILD only to recover from disaster!

Introduction to MIRROR and REBUILD

When you erase files or format a hard disk with most versions of DOS, the data in the files is not actually erased, only the records of the files' names (in the directory) and locations (in the FAT) are lost. If you have been using PCBACKUP, then you could use PCRESTOR to recover everything, but that requires more time. If that information were saved somewhere else, it could easily recover the apparently erased hard disk files. Fortunately, there is an easier way to recover from an accidentally formatted disk or deleted files...

The programs MIRROR.COM and REBUILD.COM provide protection against accidental ERASE *.*, RECOVER *.* or FORMAT of your hard disk. MIRROR will keep a backup copy of the File Allocation Table (FAT) and the root directory of your hard disk in a special hidden file. If someday the unthinkable happens, you then can use the program REBUILD to quickly rebuild the critical disk information from the special MIRROR file. REBUILD will do its best to restore your hard disk to the same state as MIRROR recorded, effectively undoing the ERASE *.* or FORMAT.

MIRROR will also optionally create a "Delete Tracking" file that will save the full file name and all clusters a file occupied before it was deleted. The Undelete option of PC Tools will be able to use this information to automatically fully recover accidentally deleted files, even if the disk was fragmented (see the Undelete section of PC Tools for more information on the "Delete Tracking" file).

AT&T, Burroughs, & Compaq computers

The DOS FORMAT program for hard disks supplied with most versions of MS–DOS does not actually erase your hard disk's data – only the Root Directory, File Allocation Table, and Boot Record. **Unfortunately, this is not true for the FORMAT command supplied with COMPAQ's MS–DOS up through version 3.2, AT&T's MS–DOS up to version 3.1, and at least some versions of the MS–DOS supplied by Burroughs.**

These versions of FORMAT.COM are destructive: They actually erase all the data on the hard disk so there is nothing left to recover. Therefore, the MIRROR and REBUILD utilities will not be able to recover from an accidental format. MIRROR will save the information, but the FORMAT.COM program will erase it before REBUILD gets a chance to recover it for you.

If you have any of these versions of MS–DOS, we strongly recommend that you replace the FORMAT.COM program with the PCFORMAT.COM supplied with PC TOOLS DELUXE. If you use this format program, you will be able to recover after an accidental format of your hard or floppy disks. If you used our PCSETUP program to install PC Tools on your hard disk, this has already been done for you.

Recovery if you haven't been using MIRROR

REBUILD can recover disks that haven't been protected by MIRROR. However, the level of protection isn't as great as REBUILD will have to reconstruct the root directory and file allocation table from scratch rather than just restoring it from previously saved data. However, if you accidentally formatted your disk with our PCFORMAT program, and you had been running COMPRESS regularly, REBUILD will be able to recover all or nearly all of your hard disk data. If you used a DOS FORMAT program, you will lose all the files in your root directory, and all the first–level subdirectories will be renamed (as the original names were lost).

REBUILD will do a much better job of recovering data from an accidental FORMAT than most other programs. Many of these programs will incorrectly build the file allocation table so your hard disk will have to be re–formatted after the recovery is done. Not only will REBUILD leave your hard disk in a usable state, it will also alert you to files that it couldn't recover properly. See the section below on REBUILD for more information.

A Note on Floppy Disk Recovery

REBUILD cannot recover from accidentally formatted floppy disks unless they were formatted with our PCFORMAT program included with your PC Tools package. See later in this chapter for more information.

Running MIRROR

MIRROR.COM backs up the root directory, File Allocation Table (FAT) and boot record each time it is run, and will optionally install a resident program that will save all deleted file information in a special "Delete Tracking" file. It should be run at least once a day and can be included in your AUTOEXEC file. This will run the program every time you turn on your computer.

To run MIRROR manually, type:

```
MIRROR   [d: d: ...]  [/1]  [/Td-nnn /Td-nnn ...]
```

Actually, all parameters shown are optional (that's what the brackets mean – they aren't part of the command and shouldn't be typed). The d: parameters are the drives you wish MIRROR to save the directory and FAT for. If not specified, MIRROR will assume the current drive. The "/1" parameter tells MIRROR to keep only the latest directory and FAT information. The last parameters are the "Delete Tracking" options, which are described later.

Normally (when the "/1" parameter is not specified), MIRROR will keep two copies of your DIRECTORY and FAT. Each time it is run, it will rename the old data and save the new. This approach allows you to recover data in the rare case the MIRROR gets inadvertently run after a FORMAT or some other disk disaster. (This can be caused by a program that goes berserk and destroys some of the root directory and/or FAT. In this case, your computer might "mostly" work, and a subsequent run of MIRROR would fill the Mirror save file with the bad information. By having two copies, you have one extra layer of insurance as you can recover data saved before the offending program was run.)

The "/Td-nnn" parameter is the "Delete Tracking" option. MIRROR will build a file that contains information on all deleted files. This will make the Undelete option of PC Tools more reliable as it won't lose the first character of the filename and can fully recover fragmented files. The "Delete Tracking" option is a small resident program that is left in memory by MIRROR. It intercepts all DOS DELETE commands and saves the file information in the special delete tracking file before the DOS DELETE command is allowed to finish.

The "T" following the "/" means enable "Delete Tracking". The "d" is the drive letter to "track". Multiple drives can be specified, each with its own /Td parameter. The "–nnn" is optional and specifies how many deleted file entries to allow. If you don't specify the "–nnn", MIRROR will create a file that will hold a number of entries based upon the type of disk being tracked. Here is a table that details for each drive type, the size of the delete tracking file and the number of deleted files each can hold:

DISK SIZE	FILE SIZE	NUMBER OF ENTRIES
360 K	5K	25
720 K	9K	50
1.2 MEG	14K	75
1.44 MEG	14K	75
20 MEG	18K	101
32 MEG	36K	202
OVER 32 MEG	55K	303

The "Delete Tracking" file is always stored in the root directory. (On partitioned hard disks, the "Delete Tracking" file is stored in the root directory of the first partition.) If the file already exists, the Delete Tracking option will add to it – existing entries will be saved. When the file is full, entries will be overwritten beginning with the oldest entries first. Therefore, with a 32 megabyte hard disk, you would always be able to recover the last 200 deleted files (assuming they hadn't been overwritten by new files).

WARNING: Don't attempt to use delete tracking on any drive that has been used with JOIN or SUBST. If assign is to be used,

MIRROR

it must be done (mode resident) <u>before</u> MIRROR is run to install delete tracking.

NOTE: If for any reason delete tracking is not able to properly save the deleted file directory information in its special file, it will beep the speaker twice. This lets you know immediately if an error has occurred.

<u>A Note on using COMPRESS with the "Delete Tracking" option:</u> Since COMPRESS works by changing file positions on your hard disk, it will invariably overwrite any deleted files. Therefore, it is very important that you Undelete any accidentally erased files BEFORE running COMPRESS. COMPRESS will clear out the Delete Tracking file when it is done, as any existing entries will no longer be recoverable.

The best way to protect your data is to make sure MIRROR is run as often as possible. One way to make sure it is run at least once a day is to put it into your AUTOEXEC file. If you used our "PCSETUP" program to install PC TOOLS DELUXE, you probably already have an AUTOEXEC file with MIRROR in it. If not, and if you don't already have an AUTOEXEC file, here's a simple way to make one:

Type **C:** and press **RETURN**
Type **CD ** and press **RETURN**
Type **COPY CON: AUTOEXEC.BAT** and press **RETURN**
Type **MIRROR C: /TC**   and press **RETURN**
press the function key **F6** and press **RETURN**

Be sure you check first to make sure you don't already have an AUTOEXEC file. If you do, this will overwrite it (not add to it). If you want to add MIRROR to your existing AUTOEXEC file, use PCSETUP or the PC Tools Word Processor to add the MIRROR line.

Since the more often you run MIRROR the safer your data will be, we suggest you also create batch files for your most important programs. For example, if you use Lotus 123, you can create a batch file that when leaving 123 will run MIRROR. Here's how (assuming your 123 files are in a subdirectory called "123"):

Type **C:** and press **RETURN**
Type **CD \123** and press **RETURN**
Type **COPY CON: L123.BAT** and press **RETURN**
Type **LOTUS** and press **RETURN**
Type **MIRROR** and press **RETURN**
press the function key **F6** and press **RETURN**

Now to start 123, type "L123" instead of "Lotus" or "123". Mirror will be run, every time you exit LOTUS 123. We suggest you create "batch" files like this for all your frequently run programs.

MIRROR

Running REBUILD

Normally, you will never run REBUILD. In fact, you should only
run it if you have accidentally formatted your hard disk, or erased
too many files to recover practically using PC Tools Deluxe's
Undelete option. Remember, running REBUILD will restore your
computer's Directory and FAT to the same state they were in
when you last ran MIRROR, so if data has been changed since
then, running it can be dangerous as this data cannot be
recovered.

If you have not recently (or ever) run MIRROR, then REBUILD will
recreate a new root directory and file allocation table based upon
the data it finds on the disk. If you accidentally formatted your
disk with a DOS FORMAT command, all root–level files will be
lost and all first–level subdirectories will be renamed (as the
names were erased by the DOS FORMAT command). If you
accidentally formatted your disk with our PCFORMAT command,
then your root–level files and subdirectory names will be
recovered by REBUILD.

NOTE: Before attempting to REBUILD a hard disk or other device
that needs a DEVICE DRIVER to run, you need to boot your
system from another device (such as a floppy drive) that has the
appropriate device driver on it and a proper CONFIG.SYS file.
Otherwise, REBUILD won't be able to properly recover data from
this device.

Running REBUILD with a MIRROR file:

To start REBUILD, type:

REBUILD C:

Where the "C:" is the hard drive you have accidentally formatted.
After printing a warning about the effects of running REBUILD
when you don't need it, REBUILD will display the time and date

that MIRROR was last run, and ask you if you want to update the system area of your drive with this information. If you answer "Y", then rebuild will proceed.

If you answer "N", REBUILD will look to see if an older MIRROR save file exists. If so, it will display the time and date for this save file and ask you if you want to update using this data. If you do, answer "Y". If you answer "N", or REBUILD could not find an older save file, it will then ask if you want to attempt to recover by scanning for subdirectories and rebuilding the directory and file allocation table based upon data found on the hard disk (see next section "Running REBUILD ... without a MIRROR file:".

The only time you will ever want to use the older MIRROR file is if you have accidentally run MIRROR again after formatting your hard disk or your hard disk data was damaged before the last time you ran MIRROR.

REBUILD will search the hard disk for the save files created by MIRROR. It searches the disk directly, so the disk does not need to be "readable" by DOS for REBUILD to work. (Don't run FDISK before running REBUILD as FDISK can destroy information not saved by MIRROR!)

Restoration of your hard disk data is automatic. When REBUILD is done, we recommend that you REBOOT your system then run the DOS CHKDSK program with the /F parameter. Any errors displayed by CHKDSK were caused by data that was written to the hard disk between the time MIRROR was last run and when REBUILD was run. CHKDSK won't recover this data for you, but it will clean up the errors. To run CHKDSK, change to your subdirectory that contains DOS and type:

CHKDSK /F

MIRROR

PC Tools Deluxe

Running REBUILD without a MIRROR file:

Note: If data does not recover properly after a hard disk "crash" it may be due to REBUILD expecting a formatted hard disk. Use PCFORMAT to format the hard disk then run REBUILD again.

If REBUILD could not find a MIRROR file to recover from, or you instructed it not to use them, it will attempt to re-create your disk root directory and FAT based upon what it finds on the disk. This process is much slower and less reliable than using a MIRROR file, but if you haven't run MIRROR, it is your only hope to recover lost data.

To recover a disk with REBUILD when you haven't previously run MIRROR, type:

```
REBUILD  C:  [/P]  [/L]  [?]
```

The first parameter is the drive letter to recover (it this case, drive C:).

The other parameters are optional and perform the following functions:

/P   Causes all output to be directed to your printer so you have a hardcopy of the entire REBUILD process. This is highly recommended.

/L   This tells REBUILD to list to the screen (and to the printer if the /P option is used) every file and subdirectory it finds. Normally, REBUILD will only list subdirectories and files that are fragmented and require input from you. CTRL-S will pause the list.

?   Prints a help screen

As REBUILD runs, it will tell you how many subdirectories it found, and if the /L option is selected, will show you all files in

126

each subdirectory. Recovery is almost completely automatic, especially if you have recently run COMPRESS.

The only time REBUILD will need input from you is when it encounters a file that appears to be fragmented. REBUILD will have no way to know where the other pieces of the file are stored on the hard disk, so it will give you the option of:

1. Truncating the file
2. Deleting the file

If you select to Truncate the file, you will in most cases recover part of your data. If the file is an important data file, and you wish to manually try to recover the data, we suggest you select to delete the file, then use PC Tools' Undelete option to attempt to recover the rest of the data (by searching for it on the disk – see the Undelete option for more information).

If REBUILD doesn't query you for a specific file, it is PROBABLY intact. The reason we say probably is that it is possible that the file was originally fragmented (for example, in two pieces) with another file that was later deleted in between. In this case, REBUILD will have no way of knowing that the deleted fragment in the middle was not part of the recovered file. In other words, while REBUILD will do the best job possible recovering your data, if you haven't been using MIRROR, the only way to know if your files are intact is to run them (programs) and look at them (data files).

MIRROR

When REBUILD is complete, your hard disk will be in a useable condition. By this, we mean that CHKDSK should not show any errors. None of your files will be cross-linked, and except for files that did not recover properly, your hard disk should be completely usable. Again, if you formatted your hard disk with DOS version 3 or higher, all programs in the root directory will be lost. If certain programs do not run, it is probably due to fragmentation that REBUILD could not discover. In this case, your only recourse is to restore them from your original floppy backups. If data files are not complete or correct, you will have to determine whether it is easier to restore from a backup that may be old, or add lost information again.

In any event, if you find yourself in this situation, we strongly recommend that you start using MIRROR and COMPRESS often so that you won't ever have to do this again!

PCFORMAT

Your PC Tools Deluxe disk includes a replacement for the DOS FORMAT.COM program called "PCFORMAT". PCFORMAT will format hard disks and floppy disks of all densities in a manner that our REBUILD program can recover from. The differences between PCFORMAT and DOS FORMAT are as follows:

DOS FORMAT –floppy disks

Will fill all sectors with F6 hex characters on every track, over–writing anything on the disk.

PCFORMAT –floppy disks

PCFORMAT will first attempt to read the entire disk. If the disk contains nothing readable, or if track 0 and track 1 are empty, PCFORMAT will overwrite every track. If the disk contains data, PCFORMAT will leave the data intact, clear the File Allocation Table, and clear the first character of every file name in the Root directory. The first character of the file name is stored in one of the reserved bytes, 16 bytes after the beginning file name in the directory. Using PCFORMAT to format a floppy disk will allow UNFORMAT to recover even the first letter of the file names. (REBUILD will not be able to recover floppy disks ·unless they were formatted with PCFORMAT).

DOS FORMAT –hard disks

Data is not actually overwritten (with most versions of DOS), only the records of the file names in the Root directory and the location of the files (File Allocation Table) are lost. Exception: Compaq DOS up through v.3.2, AT&T DOS up through 3.1 and at least some versions of the MS DOS supplied by Burroughs. These versions of DOS are destructive. They actually erase all data so there is nothing left to recover.

PCFORMAT –hard disks

Same as DOS format except PCFORMAT deletes only the first character of the file name in the Root directory (and saves this character in a reserved byte in the directory). PCFORMAT supports only high level (logical) formatting of hard disks and standard 512 byte sector size.

Getting Started

If you installed PC Tools Deluxe onto your hard disk using PCSETUP, then the DOS FORMAT command has already been renamed to FORMAT!.COM so that it won't be run. It's still there in case you should ever decide you need it, but by changing its name to FORMAT!, it won't be waiting around to wipe out your hard disk if you forget and type FORMAT. A new file, called FORMAT.BAT has been created that will run our PCFORMAT program so you won't even have to remember to type PCFORMAT instead of FORMAT.

Running PCFORMAT on Floppy Disks

PCFORMAT's "help screen" can be displayed by typing PCFORMAT ?. This will display all of the parameters recognized by PCFORMAT.

PCFORMAT allows the same options for formatting floppy disks as the DOS FORMAT command:

```
PCFORMAT d: [/S] [/1] [/8] [/V] [/4] [/N:xx] [/T:yy]
```

d: The letter of the drive you wish to format (e.g. "C:").

/S   Copies the operation system files to the disk or diskette. This is necessary if you want the disk to be "bootable".

/1   Specifies a single–sided format.

130

/8   Formats a disk with 8 sectors per track instead of the normal 9 (for 360K diskettes) or 15 (for 1.2Meg disks). This allows compatibility with older versions of DOS (pre 2.0) which only supported 8 sectors per track.

/V   Gives the disk a volume label. When the format is complete, PCFORMAT will ask you for a unique name to identify the formatted disk.

/4   Formats a 360K or 180K diskette in a 1.2 meg (high–capacity) drive. This allows use of low–capacity formats in high–capacity drives. However, disks formatted with this option in a 1.2 meg drive will not read reliably in low capacity (360K) drives.

/N:xx Specifies the number of sectors per track to format.

/T:xx Specifies the number of tracks to format.

Note: The /N and /T parameters must be used together. The sectors per track cannot be specified without also specifying the numbers of tracks to format. /N and /T are used to format a disk to less than normal capacity of the drive and are not normally used.

In addition to the format options allowed by DOS, PCFORMAT includes the following options to format a floppy diskette:

/F   Will specify a "full format". This means PCFORMAT will read the data on each track, format each track, then rewrite the data. This option is slower but will clean up marginal sector ID's. (Note: When using the /F option the File Allocation Table is cleared as usual. REBUILD still needs to be run in order to recover the data on the diskette).

/R   Will reformat and rewrite every track. The File Allocation Table, Root Directory and data will remain intact. /R will

PCFORMAT

clean up marginal sector ID's, but will make no other changes to the diskette.

Unless the /F option is selected, PCFORMAT will READ each track of the disk or diskette to be formatted to see if it has already been formatted and to make sure that no sectors have errors. If so, the next track is checked in the same manner. If a track is encountered that has errors, PCFORMAT will read all the data it can, re-format the track, then re-write the data. If a track has never been used, it will just be formatted. The root directory will be cleared in a manner that REBUILD can recover from, then an empty FAT will be written. The only data that is lost is the file allocation table, which REBUILD can recreate for you as long as the disk was recently COMPRESSed (no fragmented files).

If you select the /R (REWRITE) option, PCFORMAT will always re-format each track after it has read the original data, and will re-write it afterwards. This will clean up a disk with marginal ID fields (which is very rare) but will run much slower if you are re-formatting a previously used diskette. It will **not** clear the directory or file allocation table – existing files will be left intact.

Running PCFORMAT on Hard Disks

When using PCFORMAT to format a hard disk the only options available are:

```
PCFORMAT d: [/S] [/V]
```

d: The letter of the hard disk to be formatted.

/S   Copies the operation system files (BIOS, DOS, and COMMAND.COM) to the hard disk in order to make it bootable. Before using /S, boot the system with the same version of DOS that will be transferred to the hard disk.

/V   Allows the writing of a volume label on a hard disk.

Note: You should make sure all old copies of FORMAT.COM are removed from all your subdirectories. Even if you used PCSETUP to install PC Tools to your hard disk, you still might have copies of the DOS FORMAT.COM program in other subdirectories that PCSETUP didn't know about. Use the PC Tools "L" (Locate) command from the Disk and Special Services menu to locate all occurrences of the file "FORMAT.COM", then use the "D" (delete) option to remove them.

PCFORMAT

Chapter 7 – PC–CACHE

PC–CACHE is a program designed to speed up hard and floppy disk access by storing the most frequently used information in your computer's memory. Unlike a RAM DISK, which is dangerous as a power–outage can mean the loss of data, PC–CACHE will always keep your disk up–to–date. It speeds up programs by reducing the number of times the computer has to wait for the disk when READING commonly used information. WRITING always occurs as it does without PC–CACHE so no information can be lost.

PC–CACHE supports standard memory (up to 640K), Expanded memory (Lotus/Intel/Microsoft EMS), and Extended memory (AT style memory greater than 640K). When a cache is created in standard, expanded or extended memory, a table is created which will use some standard memory. The amount of standard memory used is determined by the size of the cache.

To install PC–CACHE, type the following (or insert it in your AUTOEXEC.BAT file). If you used PCSETUP to install PC Tools on your hard disk, this has already been done for you:

PC–CACHE's "help screen" can be displayed by typing PC–CACHE ?. This will display all of the parameters recognized by PC–CACHE.

PC–CACHE   [/Id /Id ...] [/SIZE=nnnK] or
              [/SIZEXP=nnnK] or [/SIZEXT=nnnK]

Here is a description of the various options:

/Id   Specifies a drive to IGNORE caching, where "d" is the drive letter. PC–CACHE will normally cache all drives it can find.

/SIZE=nnnK   The amount of standard memory (in 1k increments) to allocate to PC–CACHE. If no size

135

is given, PC–CACHE will default to 64K. The
maximum size is 512K.

/SIZEXP=nnnK   The amount of EXPANDED memory to allocate to
PC–CACHE.

/SIZEXT=nnnK   The amount of EXTENDED memory to allocate to
PC–CACHE. Only available on 286 and 386
processors.

Note: only one "size" option is allowed: You cannot mix
standard, expanded, and extended memory. The minimum size
that can be specified is 64K.

The PCSETUP program will set up a CACHE of 64K in standard
memory. All drives will be cached except A and B. If you want to
change this (for example, use extended or expanded memory),
use the PC Tools Word Processor to edit your AUTOEXEC.BAT
file.

Examples:

```
PC-CACHE /IA /IB /SIZE=64K
```

This creates a cache of 64K that ignores the floppy drives A and
B in standard memory.

```
PC-CACHE /SIZEXP=128K
```

This creates a cache of 128K in EXPANDED memory.

```
PC-CACHE /SIZEXT=128K
```

This creates a cache of 128K in EXTENDED memory.

Note: PC–CACHE is completely compatible with the "PC Tools
Deluxe COMPRESS program". It is safe to have PC–CACHE

resident while running COMPRESS. **(This is not true with most other caching programs.)**

If PC-CACHE doesn't seem to be minimizing disk access:

PC-CACHE will store information about the FAT and directories as well as the programs being run. Therefore, even when a program is loaded that is smaller than the cache, some disk access may still be necessary.

PC-CACHE does not currently work with drives which require device driver support (e.g. Bernoulli Box).

PC Tools Deluxe

Chapter 8 – Error Messages

These are a list of the possible error messages that may appear while using PC Tools Deluxe. They are listed under the program name that would issue them.

PC Tools

Not enough memory to handle requested disk.
PC Tools is resident. "/Rnn" must be increased.

The amount of memory required by PC Tools is governed mainly by the number of sub–directories and the number of clusters used by the sub–directory being read. If the amount of memory is insufficient, this message is issued. Use a higher "R/nnn" number when making PC Tools resident.

FAT appears to be damaged.

If the FAT does not conform to DOS standards, this message is issued. The FAT may have been damaged by another program or maybe the user inadvertently modified it with the disk edit service. You will need to correct the damaged FAT by running REBUILD.

Cluster chain in use, unable to recover this file.

Issued by Undelete. The first cluster of the file is already allocated by another file. Undelete will not be possible.

File already exists, press any key to continue.

During Undelete, the first character of a file name was requested. However, with this first character, the file name generated already exists. Another first character is required.

Automatic recovery impossible, you must use manual recovery.

During Undelete, a file was selected but the first cluster is already allocated. Automatic recovery is impossible and the user is forced to use the manual mode.

PC Tools already resident.
Residency size must be at least 64K(I.E. /R64K).
Residency size must allow at least 40K for other programs.
Residency specification is being ignored.
Insufficient memory to run PC Tools
PC Tools can only run under DOS 2.0 or higher.
PC Tools has detected SIDEKICK. PC Tools must be made resident BEFORE SIDEKICK.

These messages are issued during initialization. The user should correct any obvious problem and rerun.

Unable to use Expanded Memory.
Not enough space to build overlay file.
Overlay path is bad.
No handles for overlay file building.
Access denied to build overlay file.
Bad handle detected.
Overlay file build stopped. Unknown msg.
You can also use the /Od parameter to force the use of a different drive for the overlay file.

These messages might be issued when creating or using the overlay file. If the error occurs during initialization, you might try using another drive for the overlay file. If the error occurs during normal operations, the overlay file has become inaccessible for some reason. The most likely reason is a lack of handles. To correct this, increase the specification for the FCBS and FILES parameters in your CONFIG.SYS file. Also, if the overlay file has been deleted or modified, a problem can occur. This, of course, should be avoided.

Overlay file not found.
Overlay file error or no "handles".
Overlay file error. ESC to exit, "R" to retry

These messages are issued when an error occurs when trying to load an overlay. Something has made the file inaccessible. Most likely, the file was deleted or renamed or changed or moved.

Vectors are not as expected. Other memory–resident programs may have been loaded after PC Tools.
Removal of PC Tools may produce unpredictable results.

During the removal of PC Tools as a resident program, it was discovered that the interrupt vectors have been changed in a manner that could very likely mean that another program was made resident after PC Tools. If this is so, and you continue, unpredictable results could occur. The issuance of ASSIGN, PRINT, MODE or FASTOPEN could cause other resident programs to be installed. If this message is given, you should NOT continue, but rather reboot to regain the memory.

You may not rename the root directory
The new name is already in use
The directory is not empty
Duplicate or cannot add sub–dir
Cannot delete root directory
Cannot delete current directory
Cannot change to this path
Cannot prune at the root
Cannot perform graft

Graft would cause duplicate entries
Cannot prune current directory

These messages can be issued during directory maintenance, and indicate the reason the requested maintenance cannot be performed.

Cannot copy a high capacity diskette onto low capacity diskette drive.

Disk Copy issues this message when an attempt is made to copy a 1.2 or 1.44 Meg diskette to another drive that cannot duplicate the capacity. The same drive should be used for both Target and Source.

Invalid or unlike drives specified or must be a single drive copy.

Disk Copy issues this message when the specified drives have no chance of using the same media and capacity.

This function supports only floppy diskette drives.

Disk copy and compare only operate on floppy drives.

Error(s) detected, copy may be unusable.

During the copying of a diskette, errors were detected. The data read, even though it may be bad, was used to create the copy. This may render an unusable diskette useable in spite of the errors.

Track 0 bad, disk unusable.

Disk Format (iNitialize) can tolerate no errors on the first track. This is where all the DOS control information is stored and it must contain no errors. Errors anywhere else on the diskette can be tolerated and are recorded on the first track so those areas will never be used. This normally means the diskette is bad, but also, it may indicate a dirty disk drive. You should clean your disk drives regularly, at least once a month.

Invalid drive specified.

A function was requested that required a floppy drive. The drive letter given does not represent a floppy drive.

FILE NOT FOUND.
PATH NOT FOUND.
NO HANDLES LEFT, CHANGE CONFIG.SYS.
FILE ACCESS DENIED (directory full?)
ERROR (inv. handle–report to CPS)
ERROR (invalid access code)
Disk full, should not occur.
ERROR xx (unknown–report to CPS)
Unknown error
Bad command passed to diskette i/o
Bad address mark or drive not ready
Write attempt on protected diskette
Requested sector not found
DMA overrun on operation
Attempt to DMA across 64K boundary
Bad CRC on diskette read
Controller failure
SEEK operation failed
No response (not ready condition)
Bad request
Unknown media type
Sector not found
Printer out of paper
Write fault
Read fault
Unable to read sector

PC Tools Deluxe

These messages are issued by the general error handler. Any of these errors might occur during the execution of almost any requested function. Correct any problem that is obvious and retry the operation. Ignoring a given error should only be done when you are aware of the implications. If the error is uncorrectable, the function is terminated.

There are too many files in this directory for PC Tools to process.

Any sub–directory can expand to hold literally thousands of directory entries. PC Tools has limits (mainly memory) and will issue this message when it attempts to process a sub–directory that contains more files than it can handle.

*** I/O ERROR on read ***

During file or disk view/edit, a sector was read and the data shown represents what was read. It may be wrong. You might try to correct the data and update the sector. This action might correct the error.

Sector is in the system area – confirm update by pressing "U" ("Esc" to cancel)

Issued by the sector editor when updating a sector that is part of the Boot, FAT or the root directory. You are being given a warning to this effect and have the opportunity to change your mind.

The CPU has been tested and has been found to allow interrupts after a change to the stack segment. It should be replaced with a more recent version as it could cause random system problems.

When exiting the System Information service, the CPU is tested. All of the PC Tools programs are written such that

144

this deficiency should not cause a problem, but other programs you have may display occasional problems that can be explained no other way. These problems have been noted on some early 8088 chips.

No hard drive detected. No parking performed.

The Park service could find no hard drive with the BIOS services to park.

COMPRESS

**System reboot recommendation CAUTION!!!
CAUTION!!! Disk directories have been rewritten during
the COMPRESS function and may now conflict with
directory pointers maintained by certain memory resident
programs. If disk–oriented memory resident programs
like FASTOPEN are active, or if a disk caching subsystem
is in use, it is highly recommended that the system be
rebooted before continuing. Press any key to terminate
PC Tools COMPRESS**

*If a hard drive was compressed then this message will
appear when exiting COMPRESS. The warning is for
those systems that have memory–resident or unusual
software operating that keeps hard drive location
dependent information and fails to either refresh or flush
that information when the internal DOS "disk reset"
command is executed. An example of this is found in DOS
3.3. Its own FASTOPEN command, which keeps copies of
recently used directory entries, does not invalidate or
flush its own internal buffers when a "disk reset" is issued.
FASTOPEN does not recognize that COMPRESS has
relocated files and if the files tracked by FASTOPEN are
subsequently used, DOS gets thoroughly confused and
may destroy data. Some other disk caching programs are
also guilty of this. PC Tools own resident programs have
no incompatibility problems with COMPRESS.*

MUST BE DOS RELEASE 2.0 OR ABOVE

*PC Tools Deluxe requires the use of DOS 2.0 or higher to
work.*

PARAMETER SPECIFICATION ERROR

*The command line parameters specified were invalid.
Check them and restart.*

ORCHID TECHNOLOGY Turbo–286e mode has been detected. Your Disk(ette) files may be damaged! Slower mode is recommended for COMPRESS

Orchid technology has recommended that this particular board not be employed in its TURBO mode to run PCBACKUP, PCRESTOR or even COMPRESS. This is a limitation of the Turbo–286e board. Put the Turbo–286e board into its slow mode before running.

060 – DIRECTORY TABLE BUFFER OVERFLOWED
070 – MEMORY BLOCK TABLE OVERFLOW

These messages indicate that the drive being processed with COMPRESS may have too many files or sub-directories to process. If you see these messages, COMPRESS is not compatible with your drive. This should only occur on very large drives with alot of files (e.g. 4000 or more).

110 – MEMORY NOT AVAILABLE FOR ALLOCATION
120 – MEMORY NOT AVAILABLE FOR DIRECTORY
130 – MEMORY NOT AVAILABLE FOR BUFFERS

You need more memory or you need to remove some of your resident programs. COMPRESS can require up to 256K depending on the drive being processed. This message may also appear if there are more files on the drive than COMPRESS currently supports (e.g. 4000 or more).

SECTOR RELATED MESSAGES

200 – SECTOR nnnnn NOT FOUND
210 – NO FREE SECTORS AVAILABLE
220 – UNRECOVERABLE READ ERROR
230 – BAD CLUSTER FOUND IN FILE CHAIN

Indicates either a physical problem with the drive or a logical problem with the DOS control information. First run CHKDSK to guarantee the integrity of the logical DOS information. It may be necessary to use the /F parameter with CHKDSK to correct errors. Or use the surface scan to check the readability of the data on the drive.

320 – INVALID FILE ALLOCATION TABLE

The FAT information appears invalid. Use CHKDSK /F to correct.

550 – MIRROR.COM TERMINATED WITH ERRORS

When attempting to run MIRROR.COM, DOS could not fulfil the request due to a lack of memory or not being able to find MIRROR.COM. If memory is insufficient, you can run MIRROR by itself after exiting COMPRESS. If MIRROR.COM cannot be located, it may be because MIRROR.COM is not in the same sub-directory as COMPRESS or you have removed the disk that was used to execute COMPRESS.

600 – NO ROOT DIRECTORY FILENAMES

No files are allocated on the drive so no compression can be done.

610 – INSUFFICIENT DISK SPACE AVAILABLE

A minimum of two free clusters should be present on the disk being compressed. You may need to delete a file or move one to another disk.

620 – DISK(ETTE) ALLOCATION EXCEEDED
630 – UNATTACHED FILE CLUSTER ENCOUNTERED

Should not occur, but most likely indicates that COMPRESS found information contrary to what it expected. Run CHKDSK /F to correct any problems and rerun COMPRESS.

800 – WRITE PROTECTED DISKETTE
808 – DRIVE FAILED TO RESPOND
812 – UNKNOWN COMMAND ENCOUNTERED
816 – DATA ERROR (CRC)
824 – SEEK OPERATION FAILED
828 – UNKNOWN MEDIA TYPE
832 – REQUESTED SECTOR NOT FOUND
836 – PRINTER DOES NOT RESPOND
840 – WRITE FAULT ENCOUNTERED
844 – READ FAULT ENCOUNTERED
848 – GENERAL REQUEST FAILURE
860 – UNIDENTIFIED ERROR CODE
999 – UNIDENTIFIED MESSAGE NUMBER

These are errors passed back from DOS is response to various requests. Correct any obvious errors and rerun COMPRESS. If data errors are detected, the surface scan should be run before compressing again.

WARNING! Cross–linked files have been encountered!
WARNING! Unattached clusters have been encountered!
WARNING! DISK maintenance should be performed!
Recommend running CHKDSK /F before continuing

These messages are issued when various problems are encountered that only CHKDSK /F can cure. These are logical problems that CHKDSK is designed to sort out and fix. COMPRESS will refuse to operate on any disk that has problems of this nature.

Fragmentation encountered – compress recommended

Messages

There is definitely one or more fragmented files on the disk. Compression will reorganize the data removing the fragmentation.

Fragmentation not encountered – evaluate with ORGANIZATION ANALYSIS option

It is possible that no files are fragmented, but something may be out of place. For instance, a newly created sub-directory is located in back of the disk. Moving it to the front of the disk will aid DOS performance when searching for files.

File chain overflowed File Allocation Table

An entry in the File Allocation Table points to the next file cluster. One was discovered that points outside of the bounds of the File Allocation Table. In other words, it is invalid. Run CHKDSK /F to evaluate.

Drive not ready – press any key to retry, or Esc to cancel

Usually, this means the diskette drive door is open.

WARNING! Insufficient disk(ette) space available for COMPRESS

A minimum of two free clusters should be present on the disk being compressed. You may need to delete a file or move one to another disk

PCBACKUP / PCRESTOR

No entries found

PCBACKUP indicates that no files on the hard disk match the selection requirements necessary to be included in a backup.
During PCRESTOR, the file selection argument has been changed from its normal "*.*" and no files in this set match the specifications given.

Backup complete. Press any key to end.

The backup is finished.

Backup terminated by user. Press any key to end.

You pressed the "ESC" key to stop the backup/restore.

Backup abnormally terminated. Press any key to end

Normally accompanied with a prior message indicating the specific problem. It can also be generated by pressing Esc during the operation.

Insufficient memory available.

Both PCRESTOR and PCBACKUP need a minimum amount of conventional memory to buffer read/write requests. The main variable is the diskette media capacity. For instance, a minimum buffer entry for a 1.44 Meg media is 20K where a 180K media is 4.5K.

Skipping above file; DOS denied access. Press any key to continue.

A file was selected for backup, but when PCBACKUP attempted reading the data, DOS disallowed access. This can be due to file SHAREing or networking. If the name is not a proper DOS filename, DOS may refuse to recognize the file.

Unable to locate specified sub–directory

The user specified a particular sub–directory with which to start the backup. The sub–directory could not be located. Most likely, the name was entered incorrectly. Sub–directories with extensions in their names need a period to separate the extension from the first part of the file name.

The type of drive you are using for this backup run is not the same as was used to create the backup disks you are currently using. You should either correct the drive type by re-executing this program with the "/C" parameter or doing a full backup.

This indicates that the current configuration file, PCBACKUP.CFG, has been setup with drive characteristics different from those that created the backup disks. For instance, the current backup set may have been created with double–sided disk drives, but the current configuration calls for single–sided disks. Even though a double–sided disk drive can create both, it is mandatory that the configuration file, the current log file and the diskettes themselves all reflect the same drive characteristic information.

Attempting to position log file. Please wait...

PCBACKUP has found the current log file incomplete. This is most likely due to a power failure or rebooting during a prior run of PCBACKUP. PCBACKUP will position the file to the end of the last completed backup. If none is found, the file will be rebuilt from the start.

We were unable to position the log file or backup disk. Your choices are to exit the backup program and rename

or delete PCBACKUP.LOG or, we will delete the current
PCBACKUP.LOG and start over. To exit press "Esc". To
delete PCBACKUP.LOG and start over, press "D".

*PCBACKUP has found the current log file incomplete or is
having problems positioning the last diskette from the
prior backup run. If the wrong set of diskettes is being
used with the current log file, this problem may occur. You
may be running PCBACKUP from the wrong subdirectory and the wrong log file is being used. If you have
specified everything correctly, then you should assume
that you need to rebuild your entire backup set. It would
probably be wise to do a total backup and start with every
file backed up.*

Are you sure you want to exit the backup program?
WARNING: Directory archive indicators have been turned
off!
Reply "Y" to exit, or "N" to continue the backup.

*The Escape key has been pressed during a backup run.
Since some archive indicators have been turned off, a
subsequent incremental backup (one depending on the
archive flag for file selection) may not select a file for
backup that you might want.*

CAUTION..... If this is your first backup run or if you
have just used diskettes that have never before been
written to with PCBACKUP, it is HIGHLY recommended
that you run PCRESTOR with the verify option to ensure
the quality of the diskettes. You may not discover a bad
diskette until you really need it.

*PCBACKUP does NOT verify its write operations. There
is reasonable assurance that the technique used to record
data will detect any glaring problem during the backup
step. However, PCBACKUP cannot detect some
problems; like, was the diskette properly registered on the*

disk drive hub, is the media marginally useful, are the heads really being positioned correctly, are the heads in the floppy drive clean and writing strong. For the sake of speed, it is more efficient and quicker to allow PCBACKUP to perform as it does and when complete, run PCRESTOR using the verify option. This will read back all the data on the diskettes and compare it to the data on the hard disk. Having done this several times, you should develop a feeling of confidence in, not only PCBACKUP, but the hardware and the diskette media itself. A backup of your hard drive data is ALWAYS going to be your cheapest form of insurance. So, buy the best quality diskettes you can. Regularly clean your diskette drives, at least once a month.

You are using a color monitor. You may display in black and white or in color. To display in black and white, enter a "B", else enter "C".

Issued during configuration setup. If you want to change this setting, add "/C" during your next run of PCBACKUP to change it.

Specified drive cannot be a floppy disk.

You have asked for a floppy drive to be backed up, either specifically or by default. The total use of the floppy drives (even though a given floppy drive is not being used to create backup diskettes) is reserved by PCBACKUP. PCBACKUP cannot backup a floppy drive.

The same diskette media and capacity are not defined for both drives. Either specify only a one drive backup or specify matching drive types and/or media/capacity.

During configuration, two drives were specified, but they are not defining the same type of media and capacity. All diskettes created in a backup set must match.

The second drive must specify a different physical drive number than the first drive.

During configuration, two drives were specified, but the same physical drive was referenced. In order to perform a two drive backup, you must specify two different drives.

Are all of the drive parameters correct? (Y/N) [Y]

If you respond with "N", you will be prompted for all of the configuration information again.

Do you want to save this configuration for future use? (Y/N)

If you respond with "N", the configuration file will not be created/changed. The configuration will only be used for the current run of PCBACKUP. If a configuration file already exists, it remains as is. If you respond with "Y", the configuration file will be created or changed if it already exists.

Error detected opening configuration file.
Error detected writing configuration file.
Not enough room for the configuration file.

If you get any of these messages, delete the current configuration file, PCBACKUP.CFG, and rerun the program.

The physical drive you specified cannot be used.
Press any key to respecify this drive.

The program cannot control the physical drive specified. This may be a hardware problem, but most likely, the user specified the wrong physical drive. Physical drive 0 is almost always considered the "A" drive, but with device drivers the logical drive letter may be different.

The speed of your CPU has been checked and found to be unusually fast. It is uncertain if input/output operations can be successfully overlapped with your computer running at this speed. Normally, it is recommended to run with the /NO parameter if your computer is in the fast speed. The program will run quicker by overlapping input/output operations with the computer running at a slower speed. Press – Esc to end this program.
– "N" to operate in the No Overlap mode (/NO).
– "R" to Retry speed test if you have toggled your computer into SLOW speed.
– "I" to Ignore this warning and proceed at YOUR OWN RISK.

Many PCs now run at accelerated speeds and everything operates just fine. However, with some equipment, this "tightening of the rubber band" does not allow the Direct Memory Access (DMA) to operate with PCBACKUP. The DMA has four "pipelines" to access memory. The normal mode of operation has one of these pipelines performing memory refresh, a necessary hardware function that helps the memory remember. This occurs ALL of the time and an interruption to this process CANNOT be tolerated. You normally never have to concern yourself with this. Also, when any data is read or written to or from the floppy or hard drives, another pipeline is employed. Theoretically, all four pipelines can be operating simultaneously. In practice, only two are ever active at the same time. PCBACKUP, in order to accelerate the backup process, operates such that three of these pipelines are active at the same time. Some accelerated machines cannot tolerate three active pipelines. The resulting symptoms are totally unpredictable, but rarely, if ever, disastrous. It is not unusual in these cases to power down and back up. The user can specify /NO on the command line of either

PCBACKUP or PCRESTOR and the program will run in "No Overlap mode". Then only two pipelines will ever be active at the same time. The only drawback is that the backup runs considerably slower. If your machine is easily switchable, you should switch it to the slower mode and run the programs normally. Since both PCBACKUP and PCRESTOR are I/O intensive (waiting most of the time for disk activity to complete), they will actually run faster if overlapped activity is allowed with a slower CPU speed than to run with no overlapped activity with a faster CPU speed.

No Overlap Mode

Indicated in the upper right–hand corner. If you specified /NO on the command line, or if the program determined that is was necessary to force /NO, this message will appear. You will notice that the expected rate of data being transferred is not as high as it could be.

The 8237 DMA controller cannot sustain overlapped I/O Switching to No Overlap mode.

The program has detected a DMA (Direct Memory Access) chip that cannot be used as desired. This may be a reflection of an accelerated machine running in its fast mode. Or, it could just be that the DMA chip is bad or marginal and could stand to be replaced.

WARNING....An Orchid Technology PC Turbo 286e board has been detected and found in the "TURBO" mode. It is NOT recommended to continue. You SHOULD switch to the slower mode. If you elect to continue, you will most likely have invalid results. Press "Y" to continue at your own risk or any other key to terminate.

Messages

PC Tools Deluxe

Orchid technology has recommended that this particular board not be employed in its TURBO mode to run PCBACKUP, PCRESTOR or even COMPRESS.

The CPU has been tested and has been found to allow interrupts after a change to the stack segment. It should be replaced with a more recent version as it could cause random system problems. Press any key to continue at YOUR OWN RISK or Esc to end.

The early versions of the INTEL 8088 CPU chip had a micro–program bug. PCBACKUP and PCRESTOR both do NOT exercise instructions that would generate problems with this CPU, but other resident programs or your particular version of DOS or your ROM programs may create problems. You can most likely continue running just fine, but if problems occur, it is recommended that you replace the 8088 CPU with a more recent version of the chip.

FAT appears to be damaged

PCBACKUP requires all of the logical DOS control information to be valid and intact. PCBACKUP has detected an irregularity. The problem must be fixed before continuing.

Invalid parameter(s) specified.
Invalid parameter(s) ignored.

Parameter processing has detected invalid parameters. Some can be serious enough that the program will terminate. Some are such that they can be manually corrected on the main menu. If you are presented with the main menu after either of these messages, inspect the parameters on the main menu carefully to ensure that they are as you expect.

Drive not ready. Correct and press any key.
Seek failure. Retry? (R/Esc)
NEC failure. Retry? (R/Esc)
Read/Write error. Retry? (R/Esc)
DMA failure. Retry? (R/Esc)
Can't find sector. Retry? (R/Esc)
Media failure. Insure correct type. Retry? (R/Esc)
Remove write protect tab. Correct and press any key.
Should not occur. Notify Central Point. Retry? (R/Esc)

All of these messages occur on the bottom line only (and are not to be confused with other error messages that are presented in an overlay box or elsewhere). These reflect problems that occur with the handling of the diskettes themselves. Accompanying these messages will be a string of information on the lower right–hand part of the screen (like, "W8041010000F00102"). Normally, ust retrying the operation will allow the program to continue. If not, try a different diskette as the current diskette may have too many errors. Also, try restarting PCBACKUP by typing "PCBACKUP/C" to verify that the selections in the configuration file correctly represent the type of drives and media you are using. If this doesn't correct the problem, give us a call with the error #, version of DOS you are running and exact configuration of your computer.

Diskette is number xxx of current backup set.

You were asked to insert the next diskette to continue the backup, but PCBACKUP discovered that the diskette is part of the current set and should not be overwritten. Remove the diskette and replace it with the correct diskette.

Data error, attempting to rebuild data.

A read error occurred processing a backup diskette. Rather than reading the entire track with one read, each sector of

Messages

159

the track will be read individually. Providing only one sector per track/side is found, the data will be reconstructed with no loss of information. This will be performed twice, once for each side of he diskette. If Data Errors occur periodically during Verify and/or Restore be sure the diskettes and drives are of high quality and in good condition.

Too many errors to rebuild. Accept bad data and proceed? (Y/Esc)

PCBACKUP found more than one unreadable sector on a track/side. Those sectors with partially readable information are left as found. Those sectors that could not be found or otherwise read at all are cleared to zeroes. The danger of proceeding is that if the current function is a restore for more than one file, you may not know which has the bad data. Also, control information concerning the directory entry itself separates the files on the diskettes. This information may be invalid if you decide to proceed and PCRESTOR may not perform as you expect. If what you are doing is critical, it might be a good idea to abort the run. Then, clean your disk drives. If you have two drives, consider using /C when running PCRESTOR and specifying a single drive configuration using another drive. If your diskette drives are old, you may consider borrowing newer drives and temporarily using them (this implies your older drives should be retired or rebuilt). Again, always use the highest quality diskettes for backups.

Insert new backup diskette xxx in drive y

PCBACKUP is asking for another diskette to be inserted. The diskette should NOT be part of the current set or it will be rejected.

Insert backup diskette xxx in drive y

PCBACKUP will, when performing a partial or incremental backup, add the backup information onto the back of the current set of backup diskettes. The last diskette is requested so that the backup can continue from where it left off.

The diskette must be part of the current set

The diskette inserted is not recognized as part of the current set. Find the proper diskette and insert it.

Remove diskette from drive x

The diskette is now filled and can be removed from the drive.

Formatting + writing backup diskette xxx in drive y
Writing backup diskette xxx in drive y

Indicates that the diskette is currently being written to and should be left alone.

Insert next diskette in drive z

During a two drive backup, while writing to one diskette it is now proper to insert the next diskette in the other drive.

Data in the file shown is bad. Are you SURE you want to ignore?
"R"=retry "I"=ignore error Esc=end program

You have responded to an error message to ignore it. The error occurred when data was being read from the hard drive. The data itself is suspect and the backup will reflect a data deficiency and you are being made aware of this

*fact. A subsequent restore will include any data
deficiencies.*

FILE NOT FOUND.
PATH NOT FOUND.
NO HANDLES LEFT, CHANGE CONFIG.SYS.
FILE ACCESS DENIED (directory full?)
ERROR (inv. handle–report to CPS)
ERROR (invalid access code)
ERROR xx (unknown–report to CPS)

*These errors can occur when accessing the hard drive
itself. They normally will never occur. Those errors
concerning handles can normally be overcome by rebooting
the machine and/or changing your CONFIG.SYS file to
allow more handles with the FILES= and/or FCBS=
parameters. If you change your CONFIG.SYS file, the
machine needs to be rebooted before the changes are
recognized.*

Unknown error
Bad command passed
Bad address mark or drive not ready
Write attempt on protected disk
Requested sector not found
DMA overrun on operation
Attempt to DMA across 64K boundary
Bad CRC found
Controller failure
SEEK operation failed
No response (not ready condition)
Bad request
Unknown media type
Sector not found
Printer out of paper
Write fault
Read fault
Unable to read sector

These are a general class of errors that can be reported by DOS during processing. Some errors obviously should not occur, but are presented for completeness. You should retry operations where applicable after first correcting any obvious problem. For those errors which seem totally unrelated to the process, beware that accelerated machines can generate unpredictable results not operating with /NO. If something bizarre occurs and is not what you would expect, try rerunning the program with /NO.

Unable to open parameter file.

You have specified the use of a response file with the "@" on the command line. The file specified was not useable. Check the spelling and location of the response file.

Parameter in file exceeds 128 characters.

Each line of the response file is limited to 128 characters.

/DL parameter not valid in a response file.

This command is only valid and recognized on the command line, not inside the response file.

The size reported for this file is less than was read by PCBACKUP. PCBACKUP will abort and the directory must be fixed by running "CHKDSK /F".

All of the control information for this file including its length has already been recorded to the diskette. PCBACKUP cannot continue reading and writing the data because of this. CHKDSK will correct any size problems and then PCBACKUP will be able to run correctly.

The size reported for this file is greater than was read by PCBACKUP. Press "P" to pad the backup file with

zeroes, or "Esc" to abort the backup. It is suggested that the directory be fixed by running "CHKDSK /F".

The length recorded for this file is greater than can be read. Without upsetting any control information already recorded, the file can be padded, but when restored, the length actually written will match that the amount read. This may cause problems. A simple solution is to run CHKDSK /F and the size will be adjusted. Then PCBACKUP will run correctly.

An unexpected error occurred reading (xx).

While reading data from the hard disk, an unexpected error occurred. The actual message number given is "xx". The error is not recognized as any of the familiar and documented error codes. This should not occur.

Current disk unusable. Will attempt next disk.

During PCRESTOR, a diskette was requested but could not be properly processed. Either necessary control information was inaccessible (due to a bad diskette) or the user pressed Esc during diskette recognition. The program will now request the next diskette.

Backup disk number xxx was found instead of yyy. Press "Y" to continue with backup disk xxx instead of yyy. Press "N" to retry processing backup disk xxx.

The program requested diskette yyy but xxx was inserted instead. This may be intentional where a given diskette is missing or damaged. If this is intentional, press "Y". If you wish to really process disk yyy, insert yyy now and then press "N".

Press "Y" to terminate this verify and continue.

Escape was pressed during a verify. Respond as appropriate.

Press "Y" to truncate this file and continue.

Escape was pressed during a restore. Respond as appropriate.

Log file missing; building from backup
Please wait...

When no PCBACKUP.LOG file is present while running PCRESTOR, a temporary log file is built. This message will occur as necessary during the course of using PCRESTOR.

Unable to open the log file.
Restore terminated.

PCBACKUP.LOG was found, but could not be used. Delete PCBACKUP.LOG and restart PCRESTOR.

It appears the end of the backup file has been reached.
Should the end of the backup file be assumed? (Y/N)

This should be responded to carefully. If it occurs after an unsuccessful data reconstruction, this may reflect bad control information being processed (due to a bad diskette). If this is on what you know is the last diskette, you should probably respond with "Y". Otherwise, enter "N". This error should only occur with bad or marginal diskettes.

Is this a valid file name and length? (Y/N)

PCRESTOR has being processing a bad disk or bypassed one. It is trying to reposition itself with the data on the diskette by looking for control information. Path information when detected is readily handled, but it is possible that what appears to be file information is just random data on the diskette. If the filename and length are familiar to you, respond "Y". If you respond with "N", the search will continue.

Restore terminated by user. Press any key to end.
Restore abnormally terminated. Press any key to end.

You pressed "ESC" to end.

An invalid control separator has been detected.
Please save backup diskettes and contact CPS.

This should not occur when running PCRESTOR without a log file. Most likely this is accompanied with other error messages. It indicates that PCRESTOR is currently positioned at a point where explicit control information is expected. This was most likely generated by either the use of known bad data (when data reconstruction was unsuccessful), a bad diskette, or by incorrectly telling PCRESTOR that a particular file name and length appeared valid. Rerunning PCRESTOR with different assumptions may yield better results. If all else fails, rerun and skip the disk that causes the error. All files not on that disk will be restored.

File size mismatch. Press any key.

During verify, PCRESTOR found that the file sizes disagreed.

File not on hard drive. Press any key.

During verify PCRESTOR couldn't find a matching file on the hard disk. This is for single file operations – F3.

File not on hard drive. Press "Esc" to terminate verify operation or,
   press "I" to ignore this file
      or "A" to ignore all files not on hard drive
      or "S" to skip the rest of this set/path.
      or "T" to skip this file only.

During verify PCRESTOR couldn't find a matching file on the hard disk. This is for multi–file operations – F1 and F2.

Files not identical. Press any key.

During verify PCRESTOR found the data in the files did not match.

Cannot open file on hard drive. Press any key.

PCRESTOR could not access a file on the hard disk during a verify operation.

Verify complete.

Given upon completion of a verify operation and all files matched.

1 or more files WERE NOT successfully verified/restored.

Given upon completion of a verify operation and not all files matched.

File already exists on hard drive. Press Esc to Exit, or, press
      "R" to replace all files that already exist on hard drive,
      "W" to replace this file only,
      "S" to skip all files that already exist on hard drive, or
      "T" to skip this file only.

Given during a restore operation and a given file was found that already exists on the hard drive. Respond as appropriate.

Restore complete.

Given upon completion of a restore operation.

Insufficient space on hard drive – Restore terminated.

You are probably restoring files from another computer onto a drive that doesn't have room for them all. Either delete some existing files or select fewer files to restore.

Next path follows ...

Given only when F1 is used for either a verify or a restore operation. The path at the top reflects the current path being used even though the display can represent files from many paths. This message is given when the path changes.

Sub–directory was created.

When attempting to restore a file to a sub–directory, the sub–directory could not be found. It is automatically created. This message is given after the current set is restored.

Unable to create new sub–directory.

When attempting to restore a file to a sub–directory, the sub–directory could not be found. PCRESTOR tried to create it and couldn't. This should not occur.

Sub–directory duplicates existing file; not created.

When attempting to restore a file to a sub–directory, the sub–directory could not be found. PCRESTOR tried to create it and couldn't because there is already a file with that name. Renaming the offending subdirectory is a quick solution.

Logical read/write error.

Occurs when reading from or writing to the hard drive. It indicates a hardware problem with the given file. You can use PC Tools file verify to find and correct the problem. Or if this is a restore of a pre–existing file, you can delete the file from the hard disk, run PC Tools disk verify to mark the spot bad and restore the file normally. You can also employ the surface scan of COMPRESS.

Write error on log file. Restore terminated

Indicates a hardware problem with the hard drive. Research with file verify or COMPRESS surface scan.

The normal log file from PCBACKUP could not be opened and one was being built from the backup disks. You may want to consider continuing to build the log file to avoid the time it takes to do so the next time PCRESTOR is run. You can finish building it by pressing Ctrl-End from the menu and wait until the message "End of backup file" is shown. If you would like to continue with PCRESTOR, press "Y", else press "N" to end PCRESTOR.

Pressing Ctrl–End will search for the end of the backup diskettes. In doing so, the rest of the temporary log file will be built. When Escaping after finding the end of the backup file, you will be given the opportunity to rename the temporary file to PCBACKUP.LOG.

The normal log file from PCBACKUP could not be opened and one was successfully built from the backup disks. If this log file is saved as PCBACKUP.LOG, it may then be used by the backup and restore programs. This would eliminate the time needed to build the the log file from the backup disks. If you would like the log file just built to be saved as "PCBACKUP.LOG", press "Y", else press "N".

Normally, you would respond with "Y" unless you experienced problems or not all diskettes were used.

The type of drive you are using for this restore run is not the same as was used to create the backup disks you are currently using. You should correct the drive type by re-executing this program with the "/C" parameter.

This indicates that the current configuration file, PCBACKUP.CFG, has been setup with drive characteristics different than those that created the backup disks. For instance, the current backup set may have been created with double–sided disk drives, but the current configuration calls for single–sided disks. Even though a double–sided disk drive can create both, it is mandatory that the configuration file, the current log file and the diskettes themselves all reflect the same drive characteristic information.

Testing DMA controller...

Issued when the first diskette is processed by PCBACKUP or PCRESTOR. The DMA chip is being tested to see if it can sustain overlapped operations to both the hard disk and the floppy.

Unrecoverable diskette error. Restart? (R/Esc)

After recording data to a diskette while performing a normal integrity check, a problem on track "xx" was detected. Since this check is performed after the data was written and cannot be readily corrected, the run will be aborted and should be rerun. This problem is normally created with previously undetected hardware problems.

PC–CACHE

Installation complete.

PC–CACHE is letting you know it is now resident.

Size parameter greater than 512K. Reduced to 512K.

The maximum conventional memory allowed to be used is 512K.

Invalid or missing parameters.

The command line as entered is incorrect, check and retry.

EXTSTART must be at least 1024K.

This parameter is only used when extended memory is used by programs other than VDISK. It is assumed that you are not using IBMCACHE, even though there are no compatibility problems. If VDISK is present, PC–CACHE will use the space following VDISK and modify the VDISK header (at location 10001EH) in the same manner multiple VDISKs install themselves. If no VDISK usage is present, a dummy VDISK header will be created (the text "VDISK" will be at location 100003H). If another program is using extended memory directly following VDISK without employing a similar technique to express its allocation, problems will definitely occur. If you are aware of the locations of these other programs, you may force a buffer starting address with this parameter. It should be used with caution.

Insufficient Extended Memory available. SIZEXT or EXTSTART may be too high. Or Extended memory already allocated to VDISK or IBMCACHE or another program.

Either you have too little extended memory or it is already in use by another program.

Extended memory parameter invalid for a cpu other than a 286 or 386.

Only 286 and 386 machines can possibly have extended memory. Other processors are incapable of addressing more than 1 Meg of memory.

Unable to use Expanded Memory.

Either expanded memory is not installed or it is not available.

Insufficient Expanded Memory resources available.

The amount of expanded memory requested is not available at this time.

The following drives will be cached;
Floppy drive x, sector size 512 bytes.
Hard drive y, sector size 1024 bytes.

Upon installation, each drive to be cached is listed with its detected sector size.

MIRROR

DOS version must be 2.0 or greater.

MIRROR requires that DOS 2.0 or higher be used.

Network already installed. MIRROR cannot operate with a network.

Self–explanatory.

Expansion chassis detected. Expander card switches set at – xxxK

The above amount must equal the amount of memory in your system unit. It must NOT include the memory in your expansion unit. If you have memory in your expansion unit, the above amount must NOT agree with your total available memory (as reflected by CHKDSK or PC Tools). If the switches are set incorrectly, you will most likely corrupt the data on your disk. Just because all of your software has always run just fine, DO NOT assume the switches are correct. If in doubt, be sure your disk has been backed up and verified before you proceed. If you wish this check to be bypassed, enter "/EU" on the command line.

OK to proceed? (Y/N)

If the switches are incorrectly set, the hardware may interfere with the fetching of data to be written to the disk. This interference will change the data fetched. No errors will be reported. Only when the written data is subsequently used will the problems arise. The extent of the problem depends on the individual configuration.

MIRROR successful.

Self–explanatory.

MIRROR unsuccessful.

Self–explanatory.

Drive x could not be processed.

DOS considers this an invalid drive letter.

Drive x being processed.

The drive specified was recognized on the command line or taken by default and is being considered for the MIRROR process.

Drive x error reading system areas.

An error occurred reading either the FAT or the root directory. Run Disk Verify in PC Tools to check out the actual problem.

Drive x error writing MIRROR image file.

An error occurred writing to the MIRROR image file, MIRROR.FIL. Most likely, one of the allocated sectors is bad. Delete all MIRROR files and run Disk Verify in PC Tools to find and mark those sectors bad. Then rerun MIRROR.

Drive x error writing system areas.

Should not occur. An error occurred while updating either the FAT or the root directory. Use CHKDSK to determine the extent of any damage. CHKDSK /F may need to be used to correct the problem.

Drive x error tracking MIRROR image file.

During the course of determining the location of all of the pieces of the MIRROR image file, an error occurred. This tracking is mandatory since the location of all the pieces may not be available when running REBUILD. This should not occur. If it does, it is recommended to delete the MIRROR files with PC Tools and retry running MIRROR. The file names will be
  MIRRORSAV.FIL
  MIRROR.FIL
  MIRROR.BAK

Drive x error. Could not open MIRROR image file.

For some reason, MIRROR.FIL could not be opened. There may be too many files in the root directory (commonly restricted to 512 files on a hard disk). There may be too many files open in the system (FILES= in CONFIG.SYS too small). Perhaps, file sharing is in effect in a system with non–IBM networking.

Drive x error. Insufficient space for MIRROR image file.

Your hard disk is too full to use MIRROR without deleting some files first..

Drive x error. Control record insufficient for all info needed for this drive.

The amount of data needed to keep track of the MIRROR image file itself exceeds the space available in the first two sectors of the image file. Should not occur.

Drive x problem. The BOOT sector for this drive is incompatible with MIRROR.

A properly formatted disk should contain in the BOOT sector all the necessary information to describe the physical characteristics of the drive itself. The information disagrees with the physical characteristics as given by DOS. An old style 8 sectors per track diskette can display this tendency unless it is formatted with PC Tools Deluxe.

Drive x error. There must be a least one cluster available at the end of the hard drive. Use COMPRESS to free some space, then re-run MIRROR. If you have already run COMPRESS, then there is a file marked "HIDDEN" that is in the way.

MIRROR places its one cluster control file as close to the end of the media as possible, within the last 25% of the media. The further the found spot is from the end, the longer both MIRROR and REBUILD run. Both programs search from the back end and may be further slowed with bad sectors whether or not they are marked bad in the FAT.

Drive x error. There are no entries available in the root directory of the hard drive. Use PC Tools to erase one or more files from the root directory.

Your root directory is full. Delete or move unneeded files and retry.

Drive x error. We were unable to find the MIRROR image file in the root directory of the hard drive.

MIRROR.FIL has been created, but since its creation, MIRROR is unable to find the associated directory entry to extract necessary information. May have been deleted or renamed by another resident program.

Drive x error. Cannot update the MIRROR control file.

Should not occur. Indicates the inability to place the final descriptive information into the MIRROR control file. An

Messages

177

*unstable sector may have been used that needs to be
marked bad in the FAT. Delete all MIRROR files and run
Disk Verify with PC Tools to mark any unallocated bad
sectors in the FAT and rerun MIRROR.*

**Drive x error. There already is a MIRROR control file but
it was not located in the last 25% of the data area. It has
now been deleted and processing will continue.**

*Just an informational message. MIRRORSAV.FIL was
found in the wrong place. It may have been moved
inadvertently.*

**Drive x error. We found some data in a file allocated in
the last 1/4 of the disk that looks like our MIRROR
control file. Please correct or run COMPRESS to free
some space, then re-run MIRROR. If you have already
run COMPRESS, then there is a file marked "HIDDEN"
that is in the way.**

*The MIRROR control file signature was found in a sector
allocated to another file. If REBUILD was to be run, it
would make false assumptions based on the existence of
this sector. Most likely, MIRRORSAV.FIL has been
renamed and MIRROR cannot properly operate. Either
rename the file correctly or delete it.*

REBUILD

No drive letter specified.

REBUILD requires the drive specification.

MIRROR image file not found.

No usable MIRROR image file was found. The user may have requested a good image file be bypassed and might need to rerun REBUILD to use previously bypassed file.

The SYSTEM area of drive x has been rebuilt. You may need to reboot the system.

REBUILD has successfully run to completion. In order to use this drive as you normally would, it may be necessary to reboot to insure proper initialization of the entire system.

DOS version must be 2.0 or greater.

Self–explanatory.

Network installed. REBUILD must be run without the network.

Self–explanatory.

Drive x could not be processed.

DOS considers this an invalid drive letter.

Bad sector being bypassed.

While searching, a bad sector was encountered and is being bypassed. This may be noticeable when DOS retries the read operation.

The MIRROR image file found has inconsistent information. It cannot be used.

REBUILD is terminating. It found no useable file, but it did find what at first appeared to be a useable file, but upon closer examination of the data contained in the file, it did not seem to be useable. It is possible that the drive specified needs to be accessed through a special device driver. The user should have a bootable diskette that allows access to all drives in the configuration. Drives with non–512 byte sector sizes are a good example. Partitioned hard drives and Bernoulli Boxes are other examples. The bootable diskette with the device drivers should be used to boot the system prior to running REBUILD.

User requested termination.

Self–explanatory.

The MIRROR image file has been validated.

Preliminary validation has been performed successfully. The operation continues.

The LAST time MIRROR was used was at xx:xx on mm/dd/yy.
The PRIOR time MIRROR was used was at xx:xx on mm/dd/yy.

Indicates when one or both of the files were created.

Are you SURE you want to update the SYSTEM area of your drive x. (Y/N)

All validation is complete. REBUILD is on the verge of actually updating the BOOT, FAT and root directory.

If you wish to use the LAST file as indicated above, press "L". If you wish to use the PRIOR file as indicated above, press "P". Press ESCAPE to terminate REBUILD.

When two image files are present, you are given the choice of which to use. Normally, the LAST ("L") would be specified. If this does not provide the recovery desired. The user can rerun REBUILD and use the PRIOR ("P") file.

We were unable to find the MIRROR control file. If you want us to search for the MIRROR image file through the entire hard drive, reply "Y", else reply "N" to end REBUILD.

The MIRROR control file may have been damaged. We can still look for the MIRROR image file, but it will take a while since we must read every cluster till we find good information.

A suspected MIRROR file starting at sector xxxxx has been found. Do you wish to use this file for REBUILDing or continue searching. "Y"=Yes, use this file, "N"=No, keep searching

No MIRROR control file was found and the user indicated to search the whole disk. A suspected file was found.

The suspected MIRROR file is invalid. Continuing search.

No MIRROR control file was found and the user indicated to search the whole disk. A suspected file was found and the user wanted it used. It was found to be invalid and is being bypassed.

The file IS a BACKUP to a more recent MIRROR image file.

No MIRROR control file was found and the user indicated to search the whole disk. A suspected file was found, but it is known to be a backup image file. It may not be valid.

DELTRACK (Part of MIRROR)

Two beep tones.

Whenever Delete Tracking cannot be performed for a given deletion, the computer will beep twice. Some reasons are as follows;
  – the file to be deleted did not exist
  – the file to be deleted was a temporary or backup file (used by many word processors).
  – insufficient disk space to create a tracking file.
  – no directory entry available in the root directory.
  – access to a particular file is denied.
  – ASSIGN was used after Delete Tracking was installed.
  – a read/write error occurred trying to track the file.
  – DOS wouldn't allow updating the tracking file.

The following drives are supported;
Drive x – 25
Drive y – Default

Drive x was forced to have 25 entries by virtue of the parameters entered (i.e. /Tx–25). The number of entries used for drive y will be calculated from the following info (here, the user entered /Ty with no entry count).

for 360K or less	25	5K
720K	50	9K
1.2Meg	75	14K
1.44Meg	75	14K
less than 20Meg	101	18K
up to 32M	202	36K
Over 32M	303	55K

Other Central Point Software Products

We also sell these other disk utility and software backup products:

Copy II PC is the most complete copy program available; it's clever enough to outwit most of the newest and most advanced protection schemes available! It can also run popular software such as Lotus 1–2–3 from the hard disk without inserting the original, and eliminates the need to uninstall before doing a hard disk backup and restore. **Copy II PC** includes a disk drive speed test to help keep your drives in top shape. For IBM PC/XT/AT; PS/2 Models 30, 50, 60, and 80; some compatibles. $39.95 plus $3 shipping, $8 outside North America.

Copy II PC DELUXE OPTION BOARD

Copy II PC can backup most protected software for the IBM. (It can even run quite a few of them from your hard disk without a floppy in drive A.) But it can't backup everything. So we created the **Deluxe Option Board, hardware that lets you make floppy (only) backups of almost every program available for the IBM, as well as transfer IBM/Mac data files!**

The Option Board uses the same disk duplication technology used by software duplication firms who put the protection on in the first place. There is virtually no protection scheme the Option Board cannot handle, (except those "protected" by physically altering the disk).

The Deluxe Option Board also makes it easy for **PC's to trade data files with Macintoshes!** With the Copy II Deluxe Option Board, your computers internal 3.5" drive is transformed into a dual purpose Mac/IBM compatible drive for hundreds less!

The Deluxe Option Board will not interfere with any other hardware or software and is not needed to run the backups, only to create them.

PC Tools Deluxe

Now supports 1.2 and 1.44 Meg drives!
The Deluxe Option Board works on IBM PC/XT/AT, PS/2
Models 25 and 30**; Zenith 150, 151, 158; Compaq Deskpro,
286 Plus*, Portable*; 256K Tandy 1000*, 1000SX, 1000TX* **.
Requires one slot.
* These computers require an extra $15 cable
** These computers require specific installation procedures.
  Please specify when ordering.
Just $159 plus $5 shipping, $15 outside U.S.

Copy II for the Macintosh backs up most protected programs
for the Mac and even runs some from the hard disk without a
"key" disk. Includes MacTools, a powerful collection of disk
utilities that includes the ability to UNDELETE files from hard or
floppy disk drives. For 512K Mac, Mac SE, Mac Plus, and Mac
II, 1 or 2 drives (400K and 800K drives supported). $39.95 plus
$3 shipping, $8 outside North America.

Copy II 64/128 makes backups of most protected software for
the Commodore. For Commodore 64/128, 1 or 2 disk drives.
$39.95 plus $3 shipping, $8 outside North America.

Copy II Plus version 8 Apple users' favorite backup and disk
utility. Now includes bit copy for both 5.25" and 3.5" diskettes.
For Apple II series, Laser 128; 64K, 1 or 2 drives. $39.95 plus
$3 shipping, $8 outside North America.

We update our software products regularly to handle new
protections; updates are always available to registered owners at
a reduced price. Protection schemes change frequently so it's a
good idea to check with us if you need to back up a particular
program. To place an order or receive general information call:
(503)690-8090. For technical information call:
(503)690-8080 or write:

Central Point Software
15220 NW Greenbrier Parkway, #200
Beaverton, OR 97006

Index

K

Kilobytes written: 103

L

LABEL: 5
Left arrow keys: 15
LOCATE: 79
log file: 99, 152
Logical drive letter range:
    74
logical disk drives: 74
logical sector: 36

M

M for Move: 32
manual selection of clusters:
    65
MAPPING option: 69
marginal clusters: 90
marginal sector ID's: 131
Math Co–processor: 74
Memory available: 75
memory buffers: 9
memory expansion board:
    10
MIRROR image file: 175
Mirror: 1, 8, 57–59, 64,
    117, 119–120, 124, 174
MIRROR.COM: 118
MIRROR/REBUILD Utilities:
    93
MKDIR: 5
Modified files only: 107
Mono: 76
MOVE Files: 32

MS–DOS: 5

N

N for iNitialize: 81
No Overlap Mode: 108
No Subdirectories: 107
No Update of the archive
    flags: 107
non–contiguous file: 69
non–contiguous free space:
    89–90

O

O for cOmpare: 33, 35
offset: 36
offset numbers: 54
Operating system: 74
optimize: 4
Organization analysis: 91
overlay file: 11–13, 140–
    141
overwrite: 58

P

P for Print: 77, 85
Page down (Pg Dn) key:
    54
Page numbers: 47
Page up (Pg Up) key: 54
page footings: 47
page headings: 47
page up/down keys: 20,
    47
Parallel Ports: 74
parity sector: 104

search string display: 37, 39
sector: 2
sector number: 36
select mode: 49
Serial Ports: 74
Set Sort Options: 88
Sidekick™:   5
single–color monitor: 9
single–sided floppy disks: 70
SIZE: 88
SIZEXT: 172
Sort: 23
sort sequence: 89
sorted order: 24
source files: 32
string of bytes: 37, 39
subdirectory tree diagram: 29
SUBST: 111
Sub–Dir: 65
Surface scan: 88, 90
SYSTEM INFO option: 73
System: 22, 66, 68

T

TAB key: 48
temporary storage: 13
text characters: 39
text editor: 47
toggle: 67
Total memory: 75
total backups: 105
track status display: 35–36
TREE: 5
tree diagram: 20

tree display: 27–28
TYPE: 5

U

U for Undelete: 59
unattached file clusters: 89
UNDELETE option: 57, 139
undelete subdirectories: 65
Up arrow keys: 15

V

V for Verify: 44–45
VDISK: 172
VERIFY DISK: 45
VERIFY FILE option: 44
verify option: 104, 114
VGA: 76
VIEW/EDIT: 38
View/Edit DISK: 46
VOL: 5
volume label: 21, 41

W

W for Word Processor: 47
wildcard characters: 17, 25, 79
Word Processor: 47

X

XT: 5
xx: 131